MW00353410

EMOTIONAL
FREEDOM
TECHNIQUES

EFT
FOR
CHRISTIANS
ADVANCED

CHANGE YOUR FEELINGS,
CHANGE YOUR LIFE

SHERRIE RICE SMITH
R.N. (RETIRED), CERTIFIED EFT PRACTITIONER

True Potential
REACH THE WORLD

All Scripture quotations, unless otherwise indicated, are taken from the Holy Bible, New International Version®, NIV®. Copyright ©1973, 1978, 1984, 2011 by Biblica, Inc.™ Used by permission of Zondervan. All rights reserved worldwide. www.zondervan.com The "NIV" and "New International Version" are trademarks registered in the United States Patent and Trademark Office by Biblica, Inc.™

EMOTIONAL FREEDOM TECHNIQUES—EFT FOR CHRISTIANS ADVANCED
Change Your Feelings, Change Your Life

Cover and Interior Page design by True Potential, Inc.

ISBN: 978-1-943852-49-9 (paperback)
ISBN: 978-1-943852-50-5 (ebook)

Library of Congress Control Number: 2017941948

True Potential, Inc.
PO Box 904, Travelers Rest, SC 29690
www.truepotentialmedia.com

Printed in the United States of America.

Dedication

This book is dedicated to my Lord and Savior Jesus Christ, Who knew all my needs before I was born and guided me through it all with His precision, love, and exactness that only He can provide.

To Brad, thank you for loving me through all the times I didn't act or feel too lovable.

To my Christian EFT friends, who encouraged me and explored with me new areas in life where EFT might be helpful to others.

To Ana, an amazing gal, who helps to free me up to do things I never envisioned myself doing!

I thank you all!

TABLE OF CONTENTS

PREFACE
Disclaimer

Please read the following Disclaimer before proceeding further.

The information presented in this book, including ideas, suggestions, exercises, techniques, and other materials, is educational in nature and is provided only as general information and is not medical or psychological advice. This book is solely intended for the reader's own self-improvement and is not meant to be a substitute for medical or psychological treatment and does not replace the services of licensed health care professionals.

This book contains information regarding an innovative healing method called Emotional Freedom Techniques or EFT, which is considered part of the field of complementary and alternative medicine. EFT seeks to address stressors and imbalances within a person's energy system, as well as the energetic influence of thoughts, beliefs, and emotions on the body. EFT is intended to balance an individual's energy with a gentle tapping procedure. The prevailing premise of EFT is that the flow and balance of the body's electromagnetic and more subtle energies are important for physical, spiritual, and emotional health—and for fostering well-being.

Although EFT appears to have promising emotional, spiritual, and physical health benefits, EFT has yet to be fully researched by the Western academic, medical, and psychological communities. Therefore, EFT may be considered experimental. The reader agrees to assume and accept full responsibility for any and all risks associated with reading this book and using EFT. If the reader has any concerns or questions about whether or not to use EFT, the reader should consult with his or her licensed health care professional. If the reader inadvertently experiences any emotional distress or physical discomfort in using EFT, the reader is advised to stop and seek professional care if appropriate.

Publishing of the information contained in this book is not intended to create a client-practitioner or any other type of professional relationship between the reader and the author. The author does not make any guarantee that the reader will receive or experience the same results described in this book. Further, the author does not make any guarantee, warranty, or prediction regarding the outcome of an individual using EFT as described herein for any particular purpose or issue. While references and links to other resources are provided in good faith, the accuracy, validity, effectiveness, completeness, or usefulness of any information herein, as with any publication, cannot be guaranteed.

By continuing to read this book, the reader agrees to forever fully release, indemnify, and hold harmless, the author, and others associated with the publication of this book from any claim or liability and for any damage or injury of whatsoever kind or nature that the reader may incur, arising at any time, out of or in relation to the reader's use of the information presented in this book. If any court of law rules that any part of the Disclaimer is invalid, the Disclaimer stands as if those parts are struck out.

I purposefully refer to satan in lowercase "s." He was defeated at the Cross, leaving him bereft with no jurisdiction over our lives or emotions, thus he deserves no particular or special recognition.

BY CONTINUING TO READ THIS BOOK YOU AGREE TO ALL OF THE ABOVE

INTRODUCTION

In my previous two books on EFT, I made a case for two different ideas. In the first book, *EFT for Christians*, I explained how Emotional Freedom Techniques (EFT) is a tool that Christians can use to help them heal. In the second book, *EFT for Christians, Tapping in God's Peace and Joy*, we emphasized why Christians should use tapping as one of the tools of sanctification in order to become more like the image of Christ here on earth. With the help of the Holy Spirit, EFT can aid us to overcome sin and bad habits that keep us from walking the Christian journey as Jesus instructs. EFT can be an evangelism tool to show others how our walk in Christ is beneficial now here on Earth and later in heaven.

In this third book, *EFT for Christians Advanced*, the Holy Spirit wants to show in greater detail all of the different ways and techniques that we Christians can use EFT to allow God to heal many areas of our life. This includes our emotional, spiritual, and even our physical and mental parts.

Often we Christians begin to think we have God all figured out. He sent His Son to earth to redeem us from our sins, giving us our eternal home in heaven, and we stop there, assuming we have all that we need. In a spiritual sense (Ephesians 3:14–21), Jesus is all we need, but life here on earth often is pretty rough and tough on us. Human beings aren't always nice to one another because our sin nature gets the best of us. We say and do things that damage us and others around us in many ways. God knows this happens.

Amazingly, He understood our human plight, and He implanted in us at creation the physical mechanisms to offset that damage.

In the western world, we are the doubting Thomases of medicine (John 20:24–29). We haven't taken the Chinese holistic approach to medicine very seriously until the past four or five decades when a *New York Times* reporter returned to the States touting how wonderfully well acupuncture worked as an anesthetic when he needed emergency surgery while on a trip to China.

A movement has begun here in the West around neuroscience. As university researchers have commenced looking more closely at how acupuncture works, they are beginning to realize much of how God's physiology underpins it all. The Chinese knew acupuncture worked, and now Western science is beginning to prove why it works.

Now that science can *prove* what Chinese medicine has said all along, we, like Apostle Thomas, seem now to take these techniques seriously because *seeing is believing*!

EFT now has more than 100 scientific studies backing its efficaciousness. And it appears to work quite well on a multitude of issues. Gary Craig's, founder of the Official Gold Standard for EFT, admonition to "use it on everything" seems to be true. In EFT we must still be careful to know when medical attention is needed and when EFT can be used. I often advise to err on the conservative side and get a doctor's or psychologist's help and then tap on issues thereafter.

So I continue to write *EFT for Christians* books to motivate and encourage Christians to combine their own spiritual practices and Christian worldview with the tapping techniques themselves. It is a powerful combination for us. Drawing God closer and deeper into our lives can only facilitate a more focused connection with Him.

The Holy Spirit has given me specific visual techniques and opinions about how Christians can use tapping to heal and to make their emotional life less painful. It gives them a more positive perspective on life in general, freeing them to go preach the Gospel to the ends of the earth (Mark 16:15).

Are my words on tapping the last words to be said on the subject? Absolutely not! My hope and dream for these Christian EFT books is to stimulate others to come forward to help move EFT into the Church and into different ministries to give them the platform to dig deeper into ways EFT can be used to heal the Church and the world. Healing must begin with ourselves before we can step out to heal the world in Jesus' name.

I believe we have many other techniques and uses, and maybe even spiritual reasons, for all Christians to tap on a regular basis, combining it with their own personal practices of prayer and Scripture study. I pray those whom God motivates to stretch the boundaries of EFT into other areas will take God's push seriously in that direction.

God has led me to create different EFT resources for use by Christian tappers. Following is a list for you to peruse and pick out whatever you personally find useful and helpful in learning to tap efficiently and effectively in Christ:

My personal EFT for Christians website: http://www.eftforchristians.com/
Please note all offerings can be found on the top header menu, particularly the "resource" page. This page also has links to two EFT Facebook pages you may wish to join, along with six pages of Internet articles that explain much of the science behind why EFT works, and some of the newest research on the subject. Other resources are also available.

YouTube channel: www.youtube.com/channel/UcmxsHG9CFSWot3rDZac2rSw
Please subscribe to my EFT for Christians YouTube channel, so you don't miss any new training and informational videos as I create and publish them.

Blog: www.eftforchristian.blogspot.com
Follow my EFT for Christians blog, so you are alerted to new postings.

EFT Book Series: I highly recommend and encourage you to read the *EFT for Christians* series in the order written. These inexpensive books build one upon the other:

1. *EFT for Christians*, published in 2015 by Energy Psychology Press, ISBN 978-1604152517.

2. *EFT for Christians, Tapping into God's Peace and Joy*, published in 2016 by True Potential, ISBN 978-1-943852-35-2.

3. And now this third volume, *EFT for Christians Advanced, Change Your Feelings, Change Your Life*, published in 2017 by True Potential, ISBN 978-1-943852-49-9.

Please consider visiting my website EFTforChristians.com to order and receive autographed book copies, or navigate to Amazon from my EFTforChristians.com website to purchase books there.

I praise and thank God for each and every one of you who has encouraged me in this Christian tapping endeavor. I hope our God of mercy will shine His bright light of peace, love, joy, and healing upon your life as you step forward into His healing power as you tap and as you also teach your children and grandchildren to tap.

Please let me hear from you as to how EFT has changed your life or please email me at EFTforChristians@gmail.com to ask any questions that come to mind as you read my *EFT for Christians* book series.

In the healing power of Christ Jesus, and His Father, the Creator, and His Holy Spirit, our Comfort and Revealer, I pray for you regularly.

Sherrie Rice Smith, R.N. (Retired)
Certified EFT Practitioner
EFTforChristians.com
Author of *EFT for Christians* book series

CHAPTER 1

Sanctification Revisited

The more I use EFT the more I realize the Holy Spirit's increased role in the tapping process. He is integral to the depth of healing and breadth of completeness of this technique.

I have previously outlined some of the Holy Spirit's role in our lives, but I am intent on completing the understanding of how important He is in Emotional Freedom Techniques in this book, meaning we Christians should be relying on Him throughout our healing journey.

Jesus clearly told us He would send us the Holy Spirit to assist us through life. John 14:26 reads, "But the Advocate, the Holy Spirit, whom the Father will send in my name, will teach you all things and will remind you of everything I have said to you."

Many of you have sat through a week-long class, something heavy duty, that you truly wanted to learn, but you found yourself so completely overwhelmed about half way through the class that you began to despair. You assumed the material was too difficult and too detailed that you would never assimilate it all anyway, so why try?

Isn't Christian life similar? We learn bits here and pieces there. Sunday school teaches us some parts, our parents guide us through other chunks, and pastors impart still more nuggets. However, we still never seem to know *how* to accomplish all that the Bible instructs us to be responsible for doing. Keeping the "law" in the Old Testament was one thing; keeping the "intent" of the law that Jesus taught is quite another thing—taking us to a higher level of behavior, which holds Christians even more responsible than any Old Testament person ever imagined.

We are told to "love one another," "to forgive," and even "to turn the other cheek." I often asked what that was to look like in real everyday practice. How did I implement all that Jesus taught during his 3-year ministry on earth? Not only was I to love my neighbor, including those who hurt me, but also I was to think kind thoughts, hope and pray for my fellow man and their lives, and not complain and gossip about how awful they treated me. I was to be clean in actions and words, and also in all my thoughts. Frankly, I gave up trying too much as I saw it as an impossible task. God couldn't really be serious about this, could He? It just seemed untenable.

I knew I was one "who had been chosen according to the foreknowledge of God the Father, through the sanctifying work of the Spirit, to be obedient to Jesus Christ and sprinkled with his blood" (1 Peter 1:2). Still, how was I to forgive the people who had hurt me as Jesus required of me in John 20:23? "If you forgive anyone's sins, their sins are forgiven; if you do not forgive them, they are not forgiven."

Even though I understood my body is a temple of the Holy Spirit, as taught in 1 Corinthians 6:19, "Do you not know that your bodies are temples of the Holy Spirit, who is in you, whom you have received from God? You are not your own." How was I to live on this earth and live like Jesus taught? Life is tough. It hurts. People don't always cooperate with us no matter how good our intentions are. My mouth often got ahead of Jesus' thoughts. I pouted. I whined when I didn't get my own way. I avoided intermingling with the people of God because I felt lost and unsophisticated among them. As the pressure built, so did the pain inside. I couldn't figure out how to do life the way Scripture taught us.

Apostle Paul in Galatians 5:16 wrote, "So I say, walk by the Spirit, and you will not gratify the desires of the flesh," and he repeated something similar in Romans 8:5 when he stated, "Those who live according to the flesh have their minds set on what the flesh desires; but those who live in accordance with the Spirit have their minds set on what the Spirit desires." What did Paul mean? No one seemed able to tell me how to break the habits and thought patterns in my life, which I know disappointed God. I was in a rut, stuck. Knowing now what I didn't know then, I believe I wasn't the only one who felt this way; back then I thought I was on a solo journey and God wasn't talking much or giving me much practical advice.

I knew the Scriptures that told me what is found in 1 Corinthians 2:10: "these are the things God has revealed to us by his Spirit. The Spirit searches all things, even the deep things of God." And Romans 8:9: "You, however, are not in the realm of the flesh but are in the realm of the Spirit, if indeed the Spirit of God lives in you. And if anyone does not have the Spirit of Christ, they do not belong to Christ."

I wanted to live in the Spirit. I desired it with all my heart from the day I gave Jesus my life more than 40 years ago, making Him my Lord and Master. No matter how much self-control or willingness I thought I had, nothing seemed to help me change patterns in my life that were not Spirit-led. And it sure seemed to me I had many such habits!

My greatest desire was what Paul penned in Romans 15:13: "May the God of hope fill you with all joy and peace as you trust in him, so that you may overflow with hope by the power of the Holy Spirit." What peace? Where was the joy? I had neither. I had no idea even where to look.

Wayne Grudem writes:

> "Moreover, growth in sanctification will affect our emotions. We will see increasingly in our lives emotions such as 'love, joy, peace, patience' (Gal. 5:22). We will be able increasingly to obey Peter's command 'to abstain from the passions of the flesh that wage war against your soul' (1 Peter 2:11). We will find it increasingly true that we do not 'love the world or things in the world' (1 John 2:15), but that we, like our Savior, delight to do God's will. In ever-increasing measure we will become 'obedient from the heart' (Rom. 6:17), and we will 'put away' the negative emotions involved in 'bitterness and wrath and anger and clamor and slander' (Eph. 4:31)."[1]

Don't those passages read like a spiritual definition of EFT? We put away our old habits and ways to begin to enter into forgiveness toward others, as well as toward ourselves, with a non-judgmental attitude, taking responsibility for our actions *and* our thoughts, bringing them all into submission to the will of our Lord Jesus. As Proverbs 4:14–15 states: "Do not set foot on the path of the wicked or walk in the way of evildoers. Avoid it, do not travel on it; turn from it and go on your way." Romans 12:2 states: "Do not conform to the pattern of this world, but be transformed by the renewing of your mind. Then you will be able to test and approve what God's will is—his good, pleasing and perfect will. Galatians 6:7–9 asserts: "Do not be deceived: God cannot be mocked. A man reaps what he sows. Whoever sows to please their flesh, from the flesh will reap destruction; whoever

---

1   Grudem, *Systematic Theology*, 756.

sows to please the Spirit, from the Spirit will reap eternal life. Let us not become weary in doing good, for at the proper time we will reap a harvest if we do not give up." We are all looking for something practical to help us clean up our act in life. As a tool of sanctification, I believe EFT is the ticket.

I have come to understand that even though God and man have unequal roles in this sanctifying process, we must cooperate with God in the undertaking. God's discipline, allowing difficult and often tragic circumstances in our lives, among other situations, is part of the sanctification process. He humbles us to learn dependence on Him for our very lives.

I enjoy looking up different definitions of words in the dictionary. Dictionary.com defines *progress* with the definitions that follow, among others:

1. movement toward a goal or to a further or higher stage;

2. advancement in general;

3. growth or development; continuous improvement; and

4. the development of an individual or society in a direction considered more beneficial than and superior to the previous level.

Even though he had no idea EFT existed, Martin Luther, whose 500th anniversary of the Reformation we remember in 2017, had a comment that fits with EFT, "To *progress* is always to begin always to begin again" (Martin Luther, Commentary on Romans).

We sin, we fail, we begin again, and we *progress* and grow toward our goal of living in the fruits of the Holy Spirit. Jesus embodies all those "fruits" and so should we. This is sanctification; EFT helps in that progressive process.

Since Jesus earned the blessing of sanctification for us at the Cross, He is our example of what to strive for (1 Peter 2:21). Paul talks about what that sanctification should look like when he describes the fruits of the Holy Spirit in Galatians 5:22—love, joy, peace, forbearance, kindness, goodness, and faithfulness.

Through my decades of emotional and physical pain, God finally handed me a technique that made sense. Even better, it actually worked, breaking through the fog that surrounded my life, separating me from Him. Oh, He was always there.

My problems were my perception of what life was, what it all meant, and how I fit into the puzzle of relationships with the people around me.

It took some time, but I finally understood how the Holy Spirit was involved in my emotional EFT transformation. It is He who helps us move toward a more Christ-like attitude and life as Jesus instructed in John 15:5: "I am the vine; you are the branches. If you remain in me and I in you, you will bear much fruit; apart from me you can do nothing." Nothing delights Him more than for us to step out from under that perceptual emotional fog and move out into the light of Christ, renewing our mind and strength (Isaiah 40:31), and becoming what God the Father intended us to be from the moment we were conceived.

God does His part; we are responsible for doing ours out of gratefulness and love for what He has done for us. We have a role to play in all of this. We must not sit back, waiting for God to do it all.

Fellow saints often tell me they are praying about this or that. Praying is well and good; however, I often want to say to them, "God is waiting for you to act." Sitting on the sidelines, assuming God will do all the work is like waiting for God to put out the flames of a burning house while you stand by with a full bucket of water in your hands. It usually isn't very effective. God has His job to do; we humans have ours. God requires action on our part. He doesn't force His will on us. He gave us a brain, so we should step up and step out in faith, using that intelligence to make positive changes for His kingdom.

Grudem goes on further on that same page to outline how sanctification—the work of the Holy Spirit in us—affects us. It affects our intellect as we grow in wisdom and knowledge of God. It affects our will or decision-making ability so it comes into conformity with the will of our Father. It affects our spirit where our holiness increases, making us want to be more concerned about the affairs of God within this world. It also affects our physical body as we desire to step away from all the sins of the flesh—those behaviors that damage us, causing defilement that is anathema to the concept that we are temples of the Holy Spirit (1 Corinthians 6:19–20). Often it simply and plainly makes us sick.

God requires our thoughts and motives in this life to be pure. We are to look out for our brothers' and sisters' best interest. We are to encourage one another, not gossip. We are to pray for our friends and our enemies, asking God to bless them all. When we step into our new life in Christ, we are a new creation in Him (2 Corinthians 5:17), acting as Jesus acted—no matter what craziness was going on around Him, no matter what others said about Him, and no matter what the apostles, His friends, thought or did that detracted from His message of love and peace in the world.

Even though we are human, born of sinful parents, we know our God is right beside us every minute of every day. Zephaniah 3:17 states: "The LORD your God is with you, the Mighty Warrior who saves. He will take great delight in you; in his love he will no longer rebuke you, but will rejoice over you with singing." We are His children (1 John 3:1); He treasures us; He loves us (1 John 4:19); and He sent His only beloved Son to die on Calvary to attain for us our home in heaven through reconciliation with the Father (John 3:16).

Our Lord is sovereign in all things. He requires us to improve our behavior to conform to His will and His ways and His thoughts. It's no different than the Ten Commandments. Those aren't suggestions—as some would like us to believe. They are commandments: written requirements for Godly behavior for us to follow today.

Jesus took those Commandments even further by adding deeper layers involving love and forgiveness, making those rules even more difficult to keep.

We will never be perfect or sinless in this life (1 John 1:8), but we can move towards it as God helps us to do that. The good news—Gospel—is we have the Holy Spirit to help us. Our job is to grow more and more righteous in Christ, yielding us to the will of God for our lives (2 Corinthians 3:18). In Philippians 3, Paul talks about pressing on toward that goal. This pressing on is sanctification. We move toward Christ's likeness and toward heaven's reward of eternal life, in which, one day, we will be complete in body and spirit.

Hebrews 12:14 tells us to "make *every* effort to be holy," and James 1:22 instructs us not just to listen to God's Word, but to do what it says. Just because we cannot attain a sinless perfection and holiness in this life, it should not, by Biblical command, entice us not to try. Scripture clearly points out that it is our responsibility to walk toward a holy life with the help of the Paraclete. The more sanctified we are, the more conformed to Christ's image we will become. Sanctification is a high calling to which all us Christians should aspire.

Satan uses our senses to tempt us. Temptation is not a sin. Succumbing to the temptation is the sin. Jesus was tempted (Matthew 4:1–11). He didn't buy into satan's lies. Jesus didn't fold when enticing prospects were offered to Him. With the Holy Spirit's help, neither do we have to capitulate. We are overcomers in Christ Jesus by the power of His Spirit. He promises we will not be tempted beyond what we are able to escape (1 Corinthians 10:13). Is EFT another tool in our arsenal to help avoid sin? I know it is.

As God roots out the neuro part of our old past memories during tapping, we begin to break the old patterns that kept us bound up in the same repetitive sin. You do what you do for a behavioral reason. Let the Holy Spirit break those old behaviors by helping you deal with the emotional reasons you do them. He is faithful to help us. He wants to help us. He has given us tapping as a tool to do this work.

God's Word also has sanctifying power. Combining Scripture with tapping produces a powerful synergistic effect. God's Word bites down deep into our souls. It enlightens us about how we are to act. It gives us specifics to avoid and specifics we are to do. Tapping is the propellant that helps move things along toward the desired end, solidifying behavioral changes. Tapping and Scripture are a powerful duo God has created.

Often it is our senses that get us into trouble, and tapping helps us put them back on track as He so created them (Hebrews 4:12) to be for His glory and honor. Remember, all of this is progressive. We will never be perfect until we are translated into glory in heaven. Our job is to work to become as Christ-like as we possibly can here on earth.

Prayer is another sanctification tool. Combining prayer and EFT can often be amazingly powerful. God wants us to give Him praise and thanksgiving, but He also wants us to ask Him for favors. He loves to bless us. We are His children after all. Tapping while giving thanks can bring about a powerful healing within your body and your soul. Thanksgiving changes your physiology for the better. Negativity can kill us, literally. God created us to live in peace and joy, not doom and gloom. Once we realize all the blessings God has bestowed on us—from the tiniest bee that pollinates our food, to sufficient money in our bank account to pay our mortgage and utility bills on time, to the birth of a healthy grandchild—and we express our gratitude, God changes our perspective on life. This allows peace and joy to well up from below the surface, giving the cells of our body a great big dose of DHEA, a healing hormone. He, in that moment, calms our soul and our stress, giving our body the rest it so desperately craves.

When we tap and use supplication prayer for others, we discharge within our own body the stress we have built up around such situations as our loved one being sick, our child being in trouble, or our parent becoming senile, giving us more and more responsibility for their caretaking. When stress is decreased, the Holy Spirit opens up in our minds new possibilities for solutions and ideas, things we would otherwise never have considered, to provide new ways to deal with the problems life presents us. And more amazing is that all this is physiological, something God implanted in our bodies to help us! It's always been there. It's just that now we have been awakened to its possibilities.

As you tap and pray, ask the Holy Spirit to give you specific ideas of how to cope with a particular sin or sins in your life. First, however, confess and repent of that sin. God wants your intent to be pure. He wants to know you are sincere in ridding yourself of that sinful behavior. Repenting and tapping go together like bread and butter. You clear up that vertical relationship with your Heavenly Father, bowing to His sovereignty, humbly allowing Him to help you. God will never force change on you. Sanctification requires you to do part of the work. The beginning of that work is you wanting to change to better reflect the image of Jesus in your life.

While tapping, ask the Holy Spirit where this sin began. What was happening in your life at the time you began the bad habit? Tap away all the emotional connections to those events, whatever they are. Allow your Father to clean up—via tapping—that part of your life. Continue to repent of any other sins He reveals to you through that process. Ask the Holy Spirit what those early events meant to you. Allow Him to point out the emotional lies you buried in those events. As you tap, He will change your perspective on it all, often negating the underlying reason you feel you need to continue to commit the sin or sins of which you so desperately want to rid yourself.

All of this means obedience to God Himself. Ask Him to actively show you what He wants you to learn. Tapping allows you to go deeper into your soul where much of this information is stored. And this, too, is all physiological brain wave activity—as I have discussed in my previous books.

"Therefore, my dear friends, as you have always obeyed—not only in my presence, but now much more in my absence—continue to work out your salvation with fear and trembling," (Philippians 2:12) is your call to personal responsibility. The word *salvation* here is *soteria*, which means dealing or working through the problems of life by the help and power of the Holy Spirit; it has nothing to do with our eternal salvation as that is free through Jesus Christ's redemptive power of the Cross.

We should be striving to improve our behavior to reflect the life of Jesus. If we aren't doing so, we aren't in conformity to Scriptures. We are to shun sin (Proverbs 14:16–17). We are to walk away from it—actively. If an action is not in conformity to Scripture, we shouldn't be doing it.

Healing and growing require time and patience. It doesn't happen overnight. EFT can often help short-cut the process a little, but we must be willing to do all the work required to press on toward the prize that Paul talks about (Philippians 3:14). Heaven is our goal, but God has a high calling here on earth for each and every one of us. What is God calling you to do?

The Holy Spirit uses personal revelation during tapping. He is our Comforter, our Truth-Bearer, Who lives in us and knows us intimately. Prayer before a session brings the Holy Spirit into the tapping process, and He has never let down a client during tapping in my experience. He always reveals to them exactly what they need to know at that moment in time in order to heal a particular memory, event, or emotion.

John 14:16-18 reads, "And I will ask the Father, and He will give you another Counselor to be with you forever—the Spirit of truth. The world cannot accept him, because it neither sees him nor knows him. But you know him, for he lives with you and will be in you. I will not leave you as orphans; I will come to you."

The Holy Spirit reveals to you only what you can bear to hear or to understand. He protects us from the deep painful things of life through many implanted psychological means, such as dissociation.[2] As we tap, He is our intuition. He knows what we need to know and what we need to remember at any given time. He lets it all loose, so we heal in His timing according to His will. He clarifies God in your life as you tap out the negative perceptions you have gathered up in the basket of your mind. God then becomes alive and relevant in your life. You actually feel His love and His care for you. You want a relationship with Him, so you can know His truth as revealed in your life and in Scripture.

As you tap, ask the Holy Spirit to reveal to you specifically what you *need* to know to heal. He understands everything about you. He knows the number of hairs on

---

2   Levine, *Waking the Tiger Healing Trauma*, 136–139.

your head (Luke 12:7; Matthew 10:30), so I guarantee He knows every emotional hurt you carry.

I find it amazing that God our Father, our Creator, provided everything necessary within our physiology to heal us. As we tap, and this takes only a few minutes to accomplish, we relax our mind into an alpha brain wave state (this is discussed in depth in previous books), a meditative state, where our thinking beta brain wave state is quieted, and we can tune into hearing the Holy Spirit. Psalm 46:10 tells us to be still and know He is God.

Here, the Hebrew word for *still* is *rapa*. *Rapa* means to slacken, let down, let go, and to cease frenetic activity. Humans operate most of the time in that frenetic— maybe even frantic—mode of beta brain waves. We hop around from one activity to another, never really thinking about what we are doing or where we are going, let alone where God wants us to go, to do, or where He fits into all of it.

God wants to talk and fellowship with us. How can that happen when we have a non-stop schedule that ends at night when we finally drop dead tired into our beds?

By tapping, praying, confessing, and thanksgiving we shift ourselves to a place where God abides. Allow the Holy Spirit in that quiet place to minister to you. Allow Him to soothe you by relieving emotional pain that is interfering with your health and well-being. Let God gently point out to you where you have stepped off His path for your life.

Mark Wolynn, author of *It Didn't Start with You*, puts it this way:

> "An intellectual understanding by itself is rarely enough for a lasting shift to occur. Often, the awareness needs to be accompanied by a deeply felt visceral experience."[3]

Yes, EFT can often do this and more. The emotional fog you live in is derailing many of your relationships, and God loves us to be in relationship with one another and with Him. That is what love is about. Often with positive "deeply felt visceral experience" comes the healing. Slow down and access what is happening in your life.

---

3   Wolynn, *It Didn't Start with You*, 22.

As you deal with that emotional fog, the Holy Spirit leads you to forgiveness—forgiveness for yourself, your actions, and deeds, and forgiveness toward all others who have hurt you in the past. Forgiving another does not mean being that person's best friend. It means being non-judgmental about that person when he or she comes to mind. You no longer wish that person ill; you pray for his or her well-being—and actually mean it. You finally, once and for all, allow God His due—let Him deal with those who hurt you. Remember, until you forgive another, God tells us He can't let that deed go either for the other person (Matthew 18:18).

Not only do you free the other person in a spiritual sense, you free yourself and let go from your body's cells the pain they hold, which will most likely lead you into eventual physical illness (Matthew 18:18-20). It's a two-fold blessing—everyone wins!

The Holy Spirit can also gently point out to you the sinful part you had in those disrupted relationships. In the Lord's Prayer, we ask God to forgive us as we forgive others. What happens when we can't seem to forgive them? The way Jesus recited the prayer seems to me that God does what He says—He forgives us as we forgive others. If we don't or can't forgive, neither will He. We are required to forgive.

Tapping nearly always leads to forgiveness. It is an amazing tool for this. As the emotional pain dissipates from memories, we cannot help but forgive. We no longer feel the pull of vengeance or anger. The Holy Spirit neutralizes it.

What a powerful combination. We forgive others, God forgives us—and them—and He gives us spiritual, emotional, and physical healing all wrapped up in one EFT package.

Tapping can go even deeper. God can change your limiting beliefs around Who He is, if He truly loves you, if you believe your future home is in heaven, who you are in Him, and even other thoughts about prejudices or moral beliefs you learned from others in decades past, which still actively run your life in a way that is not glorifying to Him.

In my teaching, we have in-class modules in which we work on underlying childhood beliefs that aren't in our best interest. Beliefs like "Who do you think you are?" "Money doesn't grow on trees." "Children are seen not heard." "Big girls don't cry." "Big boys suck it up." "Only the good die young." Thousands of these clichés in families have been repeated for decades. It's part of your family history, but these mantras may not ring true to you or serve your life in a Godly manner. EFT can change these negative beliefs because tapping can change or break down our racial, religious, and ethnic prejudices. We learned these ideas from somebody. "External social forces shape our social behavior," write Jeeves and Berry.[4] Babies aren't born with prejudices or family ideals and catchphrases. Allow the Holy Spirit to also root out those ideas in your life and spirit.

What would the world look like without these prejudices? What could the Church do evangelistically if we all lived non-judgmentally towards all people like Jesus did? Tapping is a wonderful tool to assist you in letting go of these thought patterns and habits.

As sanctified Christ-like believers, we must do better than we have done. This includes me, too. The world watches what we say and what we do. If we act like other unbelievers, what reason do we give them to come alongside us in the Kingdom? We don't! If we love, we forgive, we let God handle disturbances in our life, and we heal, the world can't help but take notice.

The work of sanctification within us gives us the victory over sin in our lives. It's a continuous process, just like EFT. We progressively clear out bad habits, thoughts, and motives in our lives as the Holy Spirit ordains us to do so. Could tapping be the physiological manifestation of the spiritual sanctification in our lives? One affecting the other? Perhaps this is the unity Christ talks about. The physical and emotional affects the spiritual, and vice versa. We need a revolution in the Church to bring about positive change. Maybe EFT is the ticket we have so desired for decades.

God has prepared you for this moment in time. The Holy Spirit has readied us for healing through the trials and torment we have previously suffered (1 Corinthians 6:11). The Holy Spirit lives in you, and He has set you apart for a very specific purpose from the time you were conceived. You aren't here on earth simply to exist. God has a job for you. Have you discovered that job? If not, what is holding you from knowing? For me, it was the emotional fog I mentioned earlier in this chapter. The pain intensely blocked my spiritual sight. I had no clue.

---

4   Jeeves and Berry, *Science, Life and Christian Belief*, 216.

Is tapping a solution for you? Does God want you to try it? Is this the reason you purchased this book? Only God can answer that. Maybe now is the time to ask Him.

Following is a case study from one of my EFT students. Laurie is a Licensed Clinical Social Worker who understands well how EFT works to negate the emotions that underlie a physical problem.

AN EXAMPLE OF CHASING THE SENSATION

I completed EFT Level 1 and 2 Workshops with Sherrie Rice Smith in April 2016. I began tapping with my first client three months later.

My client canceled our 5th EFT session because she had a severe migraine headache. Although I offered to tap with her, her headache was so intense that she declined. Her headache persisted for three excruciating days.

We rescheduled the session for the following week. At the beginning of that session, my client said she hadn't had such a severe migraine headache since her dad passed away eight years ago, and she hadn't experienced a headache that lasted more than one day in many years.

From there, we briefly touched upon how she was feeling about other areas of her life since our last EFT session. She said, "I feel really neutral, like I could go either way. I could be productive and confident, or I could be absolutely frustrated and spinning my wheels."

We opened the session with prayer, asking God to guide and direct the session according to His purposes. Upon completion of the prayer, I asked my client if she had specific scriptural affirmations or Biblical Truths she wanted me to incorporate in the second half of the set-up statement when tapping on the Karate Chop point. I typically ask this question in my sessions with Christian clients, although I'm also open to modifying the set-up statement as the Holy Spirit leads.

Interestingly enough, I didn't keep a record of the specific set-up statements and the reminder phrases we used for this session in my notes. Perhaps, I wasn't prompted to do so because there is no specific "formula" we use to ensure that God will move in a particular way in an EFT session. My client later said she "had no idea what we were going to tap about" on that August afternoon. In fact, God chose to move in an area of my client's life that we weren't even tapping about!

I invited her to tune into what she was experiencing in her body as she described these feelings. She described a sensation that felt like "tension in my shoulders, neck, and head, but only up to the bridge of my nose." She continued, "I feel like I could be pulled either way." She indicated that she felt "top heavy" and that her SUDS level was an eight out of ten.

After a few short rounds of tapping, she said the level of tension in her neck, shoulders, and face up to her nose was reduced to zero. However, she said the level of tension she was experiencing from the bridge of her nose to the top of her head was at a 10.

Several short rounds later, my client said she felt as if the tension was releasing from her head, and that her SUDS level was reduced to a five out of ten.

As we tapped on this remaining sensation, she indicated that the level of tension she was experiencing increased dramatically. She said her head felt incredibly heavy, "like picking up a 10-pound sack of flour." I invited her to tune into the emotion associated with this heavy sensation, and she identified a feeling of intense sadness. She described the color of her sadness as "blueish-grayish," and related it to the "weight of her financial situation."

After a few more rounds of tapping, as we were tapping on the karate chop point, my client said her head got so heavy that she had to lean on her elbow because she felt as if she could no longer support the weight of her head. The SUDS rating for this heavy sensation was a ten out of ten.

As we continued tapping, she experienced a "pulling sensation, as if something was 'being uprooted and pulled out.'" She said, "It felt like the tension was being pulled by a pair of hands, up and out through the top of her head." She described the "pulling" as a sensation that began in her feet, traveling up through her knees, her sides, her hips, her core, her neck, and her head. By the last round, it was completely gone.

The pulling sensation was then replaced by "a completely different tingling sensation" that "moved like a sparkler." She said the second sensation was "like light, but not hot," and moved upward and through her body.

At that point, my client went on to describe her experience as "a physical sensation of something spiritual happening." She spontaneously proclaimed the tingling sensation was the "Light that dispels the darkness" and that her 30-year history of migraine headaches had been healed by the Blood of Jesus!

THE FOLLOWING IS A STATEMENT FROM MY CLIENT:

I have experienced severe migraine headaches for the past 30 years. At their worst, I was experiencing blinding pain for 3 to 5 days a month and a shadow headache for an addition 1 to 2 days. This continued for 10 of the 30 years. Roughly 8 years ago, shortly after my father's passing, my migraines became far less frequent and shorter in duration. In the last 2 years, I experienced only 4 migraines, 3 of which lasted 1 day and the pain was manageable. The last migraine was the most painful and longest lasting migraine I had in 8 years. I could not get out of bed or tolerate any light. The thought of even talking on the phone was more than I could manage. After 3 days like that, I had a shadow headache.

When Laurie and I had our next tapping session, I remember thinking, I wonder where the Lord is going to take us. I really was in a neutral state of being. There was no tension anywhere. In fact, I felt relaxed. As we moved into our tapping session, physical feelings began to take a hold on me. It was a strange experience in that my thoughts did not seem to be in line with what I was physically experiencing, almost a detached experience. While we tapped on things that have historically been triggers, my thoughts were neutral, but my body was experiencing the tension. Upon completing our session, the Lord spoke to me, stating I was healed—that my migraines are a thing of the past. It was an outward truth of a spiritual healing.

While I am still in the throes of dealing with the natural ramifications of my sin life, the Lord has freed me from the lie of that sin and the promise of that is the freedom from migraines.

Laurie Heyl, LCSW
Lheyl.lcsw@gmail.com
EFT-EnergyInMotion.com

CHAPTER 2

Using Exact Words

One of my core teaching principles as an EFT instructor and trainer is to teach student practitioners to consistently use exact words as they tap with clients. A client's words and phrases have special meaning to that specific client. His or her words may hold the perception of an event's details, including all the sensory input trapped within a distressing memory.

Example: Recently a student friend of mine, Helena, tapped with a man named Peter around an extensive list of childhood problems. She phoned me after their tapping session to "review" what she had done and to ask if I had any suggestions for their next session.

Helena relayed that Peter became very agitated when he told her a specific name his classmates had called him in high school. His SUDS on several emotions about that specific name were near 10. She asked permission from Peter and then had him start slowly and repeatedly say the specific name the other kids had called him. When Helena phoned me later, she said, "I think we said it 50 times. Guess what, with each repetition the emotional pull around that name lessened and lessened." Helena could literally hear and feel the power of the painful word diminish with each repetition.

Conversely, had Helena done this exercise without tapping, it possibly could have increased his emotional distress, and probably stuffed the pain ever deeper into his psyche.

Helena continued, "When Peter left my office, once on the street, I said the nasty name one more time to him as a test to see the effectiveness of the tapping work we had done. Peter looked at me saying, "Oh, that is so silly now. What does it matter?"

EFT did its "magic." The emotion was neutralized around the specific word, lessening the charge and changing the perception around the earlier events. This is called *memory reconsolidation*. Memory reconsolidation is recognized as a fairly new concept of unfettering, re-recording, and reorganizing neurologically the input stored within a memory. This allows the mind to form a more integrated version of the memory. In other words, the memory is neutralized, and we remember the event differently, usually more positively.

Suddenly, after a relatively short period of tapping sessions, as compared to the decades since the name calling incidents occurred, Peter's mind completely amalgamated into a more positive memory of all the situation around the original feelings of humiliation and anger.

I still stand amazed at all the stories. God is so astounding!

When tapping with others, I strongly encourage you to use "exact words."

Simply put, "exact words" is you repeating back what a client—or friend or family member—has just told you. To keep exact words orderly in my head when I tap with others, I take notes. I write down everything the client tells me, particularly names, emotions, and details of specific events or memories as they are related to me.

When I begin implementing the tapping technique into the session, I extrapolate exact words from my written notes to create my set-up statement. I may then add an appropriate Scripture or short prayer to invite God into the process, and then I use some similar reminder statements as we tap at each acupuncture point.

After a round or two of tapping, I stop to re-assess the SUDS level and to allow the client to tell me what has shifted or changed within those rounds. At this point, I get a new description from the client that now gives me more "exact words." Then off we go into subsequent rounds until the session ends.

As you pray and tap with Christian clients, be cognizant of the name they use for their Lord God. Use the name they use. You may want to ask them what that Name is after you open with prayer.

Exact words matter. Be specific with words and names, just like Helena's client Peter attached a specific meaning to the name his classmates called him in high school.

Many times clients come to you for tapping because of deep emotional pain. Often they feel no one has ever heard them or understood them throughout their entire life. By using exact words, you reinforce to them, perhaps for the first time ever, you truly are hearing what they are saying. That intent listening builds a rapport that is so very important for healing.

Another thought is what would happen if a client had a horrible father who treated her abusively? My guess is she may have issues with male authority.

If the client uses the words, "Jesus, my Savior," but you the practitioner are accustomed to speaking to the "Father" as you pray and tap, and you use that salutation, you may lose the client's attention. If she had a rough male-dominated upbringing, using your words and not hers could possibly send her off into some dissociative reaction.

We encourage clients to tell us if something we said to them during the course of the session does not sound true or bothers them. My hope is that most of the time the client will simply tell the Christian practitioner that they don't want to use the word "Father." Watch the client carefully when tapping in person or using Skype or listen attentively to the client if tapping on the telephone. If something appears amiss, ask the client what is going on. Follow the client's lead.

Eventually, with careful tapping and your sensitivity as a practitioner, tapping should neutralize the reaction as the memory's pain begins to fade, as it did with Peter's example.

However, I would never force clients to say anything they choose not to say. Most often, when I explain my reasoning for asking them to say something specific, like the name of their ex-friend, who they now claim to hate, clients tends to comply when they understand what I am asking is in their best interest.

With the principle of "exact words," be careful and sympathetic with clients. Go gently with them at all times. Be patient with the process. There are times to use those words again and again. There are also times to avoid using a word that has profound dark meanings to a client. Learn which it is and use exact words accordingly. And keep the client tapping.

As you continue to learn Emotional Freedom Techniques, I beg you to heed this call: Don't emulate those who appear on the Internet to be saying reminder statements that rise out of nowhere. This is an old technique that Gary Craig, EFT founder, called "Garbage to Gold" (GTG). Craig would literally say whatever he thought the client could possibly be thinking. On occasion he was correct; he hit upon something the client was thinking, and that was his "gold."

While the GTG technique can work, using "exact words" eliminates this hunting and pecking for issues to tap on. It makes tapping with clients much easier. In the short initial interview prior to tapping, the client will give you all the tapping fare you will ever need. Just use it! Stick to exactly what the client said unless you distinctly hear the Holy Spirit tell you otherwise, and occasionally He does do that.

I've heard EFT novices tell me some practitioners look brilliant on Internet tapping videos because they have cultivated an ability to say a different reminder statement for each acupuncture point. Well, I agree, some have a polished way of talking; however, if you've had that tapping method used on you, you will readily feel, as I do, that it makes the practitioner look showy. But it almost never resonates with you, the client, in the moment. It's literally all Hollywood flash with little substantive content. Don't be duped into thinking this is a productive method to practice EFT. It is ineffective at best, usually leaving clients feeling, once again, that no one is truly understanding or hearing them. Using GTG can be inefficient enough that you lose a client forever because they did not experience the amazing relief that EFT can offer when the technique is done well.

Frankly, emotional issues dissipate more quickly when you use clients' words, and it can also be especially easy to tap when you have a loquacious client. They give you all the reminder statements you will ever need.

My following case study illustrates "Exact Words" and the "Chase the Pain" (Sensation) Technique:

A client named Beverly came to my office feeling emotionally low and asking for help.

Per usual, I opened the session with prayer, addressing, in particular, the Holy Spirit, Who is our intuition, resource, and healer. I asked for insight into this client's specific issues.

I had Beverly tapping immediately to begin to "loosen" up the subconscious mind to let go of whatever beliefs it had accumulated over the decades of her life around her feelings. Beverly is aged 51.

I asked Beverly what she felt. She was fairly non-specific, telling me every time she thinks life is going well, it seems someone or something steps into her way.

My tapping technique is fairly simple. I use a set-up statement that includes an acceptance part based on the client's Godly beliefs. For Beverly, it went as follows: "Even though I have this belief that no one helps me, I choose to believe when Scripture says God will never leave me or forsake me, knowing God loves me just the way I am, and I accept myself the way I am, too."

We tapped two rounds with this the reminder statement: "No one helps me." I then stopped to inquire further.

"Where do you feel in your body this 'something or someone steps into my way'?" I inquired.

"It's in my throat," she answered. I replied, "What does your throat feel like to you right now as we sit here?" Her description: "It's tightened like someone is strangling me."

I inquired about her SUDS level in order to gauge what she perceived this feeling to be and to teach her what it would feel like when the SUDS level dropped to a zero! She informed me the strangling, tightening feeling was an 8. We began to tap.

Now, watch carefully as this narrative plays out, showing how the subconscious mind intertwines our conscious thoughts with bodily sensations. The entire session lasted 90 minutes, so I am writing about the highlights only as it all unfolded during Beverly's visit.

Set-up statement: "Even though I have tight, strangling feeling in my throat, I know God loves me and therefore I accept myself just the way I am." We tapped two rounds on the reminder statement, "Tight and strangling" and "someone (or something) steps into my way."

As we continued to talk briefly and tap, I asked her how the strangling feeling felt now. Beverly said, "I'm always hung out there alone." I knew she didn't hear her own words, so I repeated them back to her. This is one of the many "aha" moments she was to have in this session. No wonder she felt like she was strangling!

I set up the comment and we tapped two rounds on "I'm always hung out alone."

The strangling feeling dropped to a zero SUDS.

I asked Beverly what she now felt. What else in her body was trying to talk to her? She informed me that her left eye hurt, underneath on the orbit. Her SUDS was a 5 on that discomfort, so once again I set-up the tapping with her description: "Even though my left eye orbit bone hurts, feeling like a deep ache, way down inside my head, I know that God is my Hope and Salvation, and He always has a plan for my life."

We tapped a couple of rounds on the deep ache in her left eye until the SUDS dropped to a 2.

I watched as a stunned look came over Beverly's face. I asked her what she was thinking. "No one holds me up in anything I do. I have no support," she told me. "Doesn't the orbit of the eye support the eyeball itself?" she asked. Yes, it does!

We tapped two more rounds on "This remaining lack of support," and her aching left orbit dropped out at a zero.

The EFT technique I was using here is called "Chase the Pain." In this case, it was closer to "Chase the Sensation" as not everything Beverly was feeling was actual pain. The prevailing thought here is that each different bodily sensation is actually a different aspect of an emotional issue. Remember, an aspect is a detail, usually sensory (that can literally be almost anything), of a negative memory or event we hold in a body part. An aspect fleshes out the memory, making it specific to us in our own mind, experience, and perception. Remember: The mind is the body; the body is the mind! We hold our memories in our body's cells.

I could have just as easily used a different technique called "Tell the Story" by asking Beverly to give me the earliest memories she had of not feeling supported or helped. I would have had her relate to me in specific detail all that happened in those early memories, one by one. The tapping would most likely have negated the emotional control of the specific memories, helping Beverly to move beyond the thought that "no one helps me."

"Chase the Pain" Technique is gentler because the client need not recall the emotional suffering involved in some negative, heart-rending memory.

Beverly and I continued to tap.

I asked her to close her eye—which were now without the aching!—and look at the dark area behind them, allowing her mind to clear, asking the Holy Spirit what else she felt in the moment. Sometimes, here I have the client do a body scan whereby he or she slowly checks from the top of the head to the soles of the feet, looking for any sensation that seems to be out of place or unusual.

"I feel something in my right inner elbow," she related to me. I inquired as to exactly what that felt like. "It's a pulling sensation, a stretching. It doesn't feel pleasant at all," Beverly explained.

Once again, I set up the tapping with those details along with an appropriate scriptural acceptance statement, and we tapped on her 7 SUDS elbow sensation.

After a round of tapping, I could see something change in her face. We stopped tapping, and I inquired what she was thinking. "This is weird, but the thought came to me that I am always out there swinging alone!" she told me. I smiled. She continued, "And that is exactly what my elbow feels like—someone has me hanging at the end of a rope by my left arm pulling on it! That is amazing!"

It is indeed amazing! The subconscious is very often literal! Beverly was beginning to cultivate a sense of mindfulness—an understanding of how her emotions impact her physical feelings and likely her health.

"Let's keep going," I told her, "so go feel into your body and tell me what else isn't just right."

"Right now, I feel a zinger down my right calf," she related. "I get these once in a while, but I have no idea what they are."

"Describe the 'zinger' to me," I asked her. "It feels like an electrical current shooting down the inside of my right calf, from the back of my knee to the inside of my ankle. It stops there," she described.

Again, I set up the tapping round with the appropriate details based on what Beverly just described. We tapped 2 rounds on it.

"What do you think this zinger means or wants to tell you?" I inquired. "Does it have a message for you? Or does the Holy Spirit have something to say about it?"

Beverly continued to slowly tap on her thymus point, looked up at me, grinning, and said, "This is funny, you know, but I've never felt anyone has ever stood up for me."

I grinned back and asked how she felt about that now.

"That is not true. I have had many people stand up for me in years past. I see some of it now. I remember Mrs. Schmid, my teacher in 5th grade. She got me out of hot water with the principal. My aunt stood up for me when Mom blamed me for breaking her favorite vase when my brother was actually responsible. And just recently my husband went to bat for me with the church council when they were discussing whether or not to shut down a food pantry

project I had started two years ago; they let it ride for another year when they will take another look at it again."

"Thinking that no one helps me seems to be more of a thought in my head than anything really based in reality. This has been amazingly helpful. I thank you for tapping with me," Beverly concluded.

When tapping, you should never underestimate the power of clients' words! And because clients' words are so important to them, remember to use their EXACT words when tapping. Those words have a specific meaning to their subconscious mind.

As coaches, we don't make word connections for clients. We allow clients to connect together their own meaning and words. Allow them to change their own neural pathways around their own experiences and memories. We call this a cognitive shift. Often, leading clients to remember a memory, and with each retelling they change the neural pathways to it and the story line around it—memory reconsolidation—that will bring forth an emotional healing for clients.

CHAPTER 3

Taking Thoughts Captive

"The weapons we fight with are not the weapons of the world. On the contrary, they have divine power to demolish strongholds. We demolish arguments and every pretension that sets itself up against the knowledge of God, and we take captive every thought to make it obedient to Christ." (2 Corinthians 10:4–5)

We've heard many sermons on these two verses over the years. But how many times has the preacher instructed you on HOW to accomplish this action that Apostle Paul talks about? Over the years, I have been frustrated at the end of a sermon knowing no more than I did at the beginning!

Paul was obviously speaking to the Corinthians who prided themselves on their philosophical discussions. They depended on their deep human thinking. God wasn't on their radar and Paul planned to set them straight on Who our God is. Paul was asking the Holy Spirit to intervene while he talked. Why? Because the Holy Spirit has God's perspective on what is happening around us at all times.

By gaining God's perspective on all things, we, too, can have the mind of Christ. We can, in our humanness, demolish our wrong thinking that clouds our human perspective.

We know what right thinking is because God has laid all that out in His Holy Word—Scriptures. He handed Moses the Ten Commandments on Mount Sinai millennia ago. Those commandments are specific. They are God's particular and peculiar way of living.

When Jesus came to earth over 2000 years ago, He redeemed us. We believers now have a place in heaven for eternity based on what He did on Calvary, but His death doesn't negate His desire that we lead a righteous as possible life for Him. In fact, because He died for us, we WANT to live a moral, Godly life simply because of what He did for us on that Cross. We should be thankful that our God willingly gave up His earthly life for our eternal salvation.

Let me share a story with you. Marilyn, age 44, was raised in the Church since she was a child. She attended Sunday school regularly, but Marilyn was still bound up in insecurity and fear based mostly on how she thought other people saw her. No matter how much volunteering Marilyn did at church, it never seemed to be enough in her mind. She felt compelled to work harder, hoping someone in the building would notice all she accomplished. Perfection was her goal.

Perfection, in human terms, does not exist. Only one perfect human, Jesus Christ, ever existed—a sinless man Who performed flawlessly all that His Father required of Him. We humans can never hope to obtain this level of perfection. God requires that we do our best, but we will never see perfection this side of heaven.

In her head, Marilyn knew that God looked upon her as perfect because of Jesus' work. Marilyn's upbringing sent her in this direction. Her father was usually absent from home in her early years because of his work schedule. He paid little attention to Marilyn when he was around. When he spoke to her, it was usually in a demeaning way—discouraging to her.

This taught Marilyn to be a people pleaser. She looked to others for her source of strength and to reinforce to herself that she had worth in this world. If someone appeared displeased with her in any way, her world fell apart emotionally. All Marilyn wanted was acceptance from someone in her life.

When Marilyn gave her life to Christ when she was 23, she hoped down deep the severity of her acceptance problem would melt away as she became more and more involved in the congregation. It never happened. Soon, her problem with acceptance arose in church as it had with her dad; no one seemed to even notice her.

Her new-found belief in Christ didn't sink far enough to her heart to change her thinking patterns. She wanted to be liked and noticed, hoping for someone to love her for who she was.

Satan had deceived Marilyn into thinking that acceptance by others was equal to acceptance by Christ. We know satan is the master of lies. He keeps us locked up within ourselves, feeling damaged and alone, manipulating our thoughts away from our Savior.

Satan uses our early life experiences to accomplish this, molding them negatively. If we had any kind of early childhood distress, he keeps us bound up in that emotional pain, trapping us in our way of thinking. We are told by Apostle Paul to renew our minds in Christ (Romans 12:2).

This is where the rubber hits the road. If it were easy to demolish those negative thoughts of who we are in Christ, the ones holding us prisoner in our own mind, then all Christians would be free, healthy and joyful.

It's the knowing WHO we are and to WHOM we belong that sets us free to do the will of the Father here on earth.

Most of us, like Marilyn, can't break down that pattern of living that has built up since childhood.

Proverbs 29:25 reads, "Fear of man will prove to be a snare, but whoever trusts in the LORD is kept safe." Most of us live in the "fear of man." We say and do whatever it is we think those around us want us to do or to say. When we lose sight of to Whom we belong, we open ourselves up to deception and a life of bondage to the thoughts and whims of others.

Eve did that in the Garden of Eden. She forgot who the Master of the Garden was. She forgot Who owned the Garden and Who created her and her living space, succumbing to the distorted thoughts of the serpent who twisted God's words when he spoke to Eve.

Our human mind twists our thoughts and the words of others to mean something other than what was actually spoken. This is perception. In the moment, we perceive something that is not there at all. We are deceived by our own thinking. We begin to second-guess our thoughts, motives, and actions. We tie ourselves in knots, worrying and wondering if all our life efforts are correct. Anxiousness takes over, and we allow other flawed humans to run our life through their opinions of who we are and what we do.

By uncovering false perceptions through tapping, all the lies we tell ourselves are revealed—lies the enemy loves to perpetuate in our thought process: "I must be perfect to be accepted," "I must care for everyone and everything because that is what God's Word says," "I must earn God's love and struggle through life," and even more insidious thoughts like "Does God really care?" or "Does God really love me since nothing is working out well in my life?"

These questions lead to all kinds of negative thinking that, in turn, often lead us to doubt who we are in Christ. When we have no solution to undo these thoughts, we often stop thinking and praying and start doing—doing whatever it takes to keep us from feeling unworthy or unloved.

Behaviors like self-medication, alcohol, drugs, gossip, worry, rage, porn, adultery, gambling, and excessive shopping, to name a few, all pop up as numbing-out diversions that keep us from moving forward in Christ. These are our coping mechanisms that come from our human side, which we use to fight satan's lies. We use these defensive behaviors to make us feel better about ourselves or perhaps not to think about what or who we detest in our lives.

Marilyn became overly focused on herself and everything about her life. Her incessant thinking made her analyze her choices and actions. She questioned herself and her own thought process, and it controlled her every move in her private and public life.

Again, we can see satan's deceitfulness here in full bloom. He convinces us that we can never think or act like Jesus. So why try?

Here is where God's amazing power of EFT can enter the scene!

God implanted in us an amazing ability to change our mind. Over the past two decades, scientific research has shown that what seemed impossible is quite possible. Our brain, as God created it, has neuroplasticity. It can change at any age or stage in life. Neuroplasticity means we can learn new things anytime we choose to learn them. Our brain can indeed adapt to change our thoughts, which can then change our life.[5]

Most of the time, positive thoughts alone—repetitively done or not—make it nearly impossible to change our behavior. Our subconscious mind runs 97% to 99% of our thought life.[6] The subconscious mind wants our behavior to remain

---

5   Leaf, *How to Switch on Your Brain*, 30.
6   Lipton, *The Biology of Belief*, 33.

status quo. It hates change. It often hardwires our chemical make-up to keep that negative behavior intact.

However, God implanted in us a system that appears to override that hardwired permanent neurology that creates a feeling of being stuck in life in a place where we don't want to be.

In the past two decades, modern research suggests that by using some energy modality, EFT in particular, we can change our neural pathways, thus rewiring our behaviors to conform to the image of Christ.

EFT is responsibility based. We must realize somewhere along the line that life isn't working out the way we know God wants it to work. We know we are responsible for our behavior. The Holy Spirit is our help when we choose to change, but God won't force change on us. He will allow circumstances to occur to encourage us to make better choices, but He doesn't make life go badly to force that change.

Much of the time, circumstances happen because we have chosen poorly from the start. We gamble and lose all our money, we eat too much of the wrong foods and suffer from disease, we try drugs and become addicts, we drive our car too fast and get into an accident, we try sex outside marriage and get pregnant. But sometimes, things happen to us in life that weren't our choice. We are abused physically, emotionally, or sexually as a child, a civil war begins around us and our family is wiped out, a devastating hurricane shows up to destroy everything we own, a loved one dies unexpectedly and it permanently changes life as we know it.

Of all these occurrences—the ones we chose or those foisted on us—we create a story around the incident. We create details about what we perceived the incident meant to us, and what it said about who we are as humans and as a child of God. Perhaps we decided there was no God, or He didn't care, or He wouldn't have allowed these problems to happen.

Such perceptions can play out for years or decades in our lives until one day we realize the thoughts aren't helping us with what we think we should have or getting us what we want. We decide there must be a better way to live, and we step out to look for help to get us out of this inadequate mindset.

EFT is a tool that can help neutralize your negative behaviors from past events and memories from your neurology. EFT can help clear it all out once and for all, allowing you to step into the future that God has already ordained for you. It now gives you the luxury of thinking about other solutions to issues in your life, rather than simply reacting to what is happening around you. It frees you from the repetitive behavior of allowing others to run your life because you interpret what and how they say things in the same old way—again and again.

Now that you are willing to assume responsibility, confessing and repenting of your negative thoughts allows you to take those thoughts captive for Christ. You then turn them around to become who God wants you to be, joining His team. He can now use you for His Kingdom's advancement because you are focused on Him, not on yourself. You turn your behavior around 180 degrees from self-advancement to Kingdom advancement. No longer are you the rear-guard looking backward. Now God can attach you to His scouting team, one that is out looking for new and novel ways to move His Kingdom forward!

With the Holy Spirit's assistance, you now can focus your thoughts on Jesus Himself, the Author and Finisher of our faith. Philippians 4:8 talks about, "whatever is true, whatever is noble, whatever is right, whatever is pure, whatever is lovely, whatever is admirable—if anything is excellent or praiseworthy—think about such things." You will begin to see old behaviors melt away. Television shows you once thought impossible to live without watching will no longer interest you. Weekend activities that dominated your life for decades will slowly drift further and further from your mind, as God rewires your mind in His direction.

Some of this turning around—the definition of repentance—revolves around our human pride issue. We Americans, in particular, often tout our "can do" attitude. Tapping often shows us where those thought patterns are faulty. We think we have been wronged by everyone. Wallowing in self-pity and victimhood, we cannot see the behavior. It's a matter of feeling stuck and unable to move out of an attitude that has held us fast for decades.

Dr. Caroline Leaf states this point:

> "Faith and fear are not just emotions, but spiritual forces with chemicals and electrical representation in the body. Consequently they directly impact bodily functions. Every emotion results in an attitude. An attitude is a state of mind that produces a reaction in the body and a resultant behavior."[7]

---

7   Leaf, *Who Switched off My Brain?*, 19-20.

We think we are in control of our life. But in reality, we have relinquished control to the enemy since he has our feet stuck fast in a quagmire of these emotions and attitudes, many of which are simply our early perceptions. We are useless to the Kingdom.

Oftentimes, Christians are like the man lying beside the pool at Bethesda for almost 40 years. The story plays out in John chapter 5 where Jesus asks the man if he wants to be made whole. The question sounds obviously inane. The man has been there for decades, so he must want to be healed, right? So why didn't that happen? Perhaps the man really didn't want to be healed.

Was he getting something positive out of continuing to be sick—secondary gain whereby we tend to be more comfortable with a known problem than with an unknown solution—? Food? Attention? What was this particular man's bright spot in staying ill? It must have been something or he would have dropped his pride to ask someone nearby to help him into the pool when the angel stirred the waters.

We, too, often act just like this man at the Bethesda pool. It's easier to stay ill or emotionally stuck than muster the energy to try something else. Sometimes, we just can't see another solution. That was my personal *modus operandi* for years.

Just like splashing around in a pool expecting healing, EFT looks ridiculous! Tapping on my face and body parts are going to help me heal? This might be the way our Lord breaks down the power of pride in our lives. He always uses the simplest, seemingly inconsequential thing to bring salvation to us. He sent Jesus, as a wee baby, to save the entire world. It cannot get much simpler than that.

Take a chance on tapping. Hire an EFT practitioner to help you learn how to best dismantle behaviors in your life that are disappointing to our God and useless to Him and you in bringing His Kingdom to earth today.

Learn to bring every thought captive to Christ. Through God's created physiology, He just may have a healing in store for you. Take those impure disobedient thoughts to Jesus, allowing Him to turn them around to obedience to Him.

CHAPTER 4

Emotion Scriptures

Christian EFT has specific language, and the use of that language differs greatly from that of general Clinical EFT as demonstrated on the Internet and in most YouTube videos.

As a matter of personal choice, I don't advocate the use of tapping scripts or tapping to YouTube videos other than for general use and to learn how to tap and only if the person presenting the video is well versed and knowledgeable in EFT techniques. There are many variations out there. As a trained professional, however, I recommend my YouTube videos as instructional videos. Learn to tap for yourself, as specificity tends to promote the best personal healing: https://www.youtube.com/channel/UcmxsHG9CFSWot3rDZac2rSw

Please feel free to subscribe to my YouTube channel, so you are notified whenever I release a new Christian EFT video.

EFT has been in practice for nearly 25 years, and EFT has undergone many technique revisions. *See EFT for Christians Video #24:* https://www.youtube.com/watch?v=p-9rl0SuuHA

In the beginning, we used the "full basic recipe" for tapping, which included the face, body, hand points, and the Nine Gamut Routine. *See EFT for Christians Video #10:* https://www.youtube.com/watch?v=52GsyvzVJ1k&t=5s

Later advocates of EFT found shortening the "full basic recipe" did not appear to diminish the efficacy of EFT. We now call this shorter technique the "shortcut recipe" or "Short Basic Recipe". This shorter version takes out two elements—tapping on the finger points and the Nine Gamut Routine.

With the Short Basic Recipe, the finger points were eliminated for good reason. The body has 12–14 main meridians. These microtubules crisscross the body, running alongside the blood vessels and lymphatic system, and they seem to carry some bio-electrical energy to every organ and body part. These meridians have apparently been found by research to exist. See http://www.ewao.com/a/science-finally-proves-meridians-exist-2/ for details. Because we use the fingertips of either hand while tapping the set-up and during the tapping round, we are stimulating those finger points. Therefore, for efficiency, there is no need for redundancy. However, if you find that using the fingertip tapping points to be more effective in your personal tapping, by all means feel free to use them! All of us have a favorite tapping point on our body, and I highly encourage you to use that particular point because it is most probably an area where your body knows you have meridian congestion, and that spot needs extra attention.

Over the past two decades, Emotional Freedom Techniques proponents have made a concerted effort to research tapping. To date, more than 100 studies have shown the efficacy of EFT. EFT Universe has a webpage devoted to outlining many of these studies. See http://www.eftuniverse.com/research-studies/eft-research for details. I have a YouTube video #8 where I, too, give a short explanation of a few EFT research studies. See https://www.youtube.com/watch?v=Wbfuw76bqBc&t=17s. The tapping technique I advocate and use in my YouTube videos is the technique used in most of this research. In other words, it is a tried and proven way to tap, so why invent a different technique if one already exists that works well.

All that said some people do use a tapping variation. If you feel a variation of EFT works better for you, please use it. Tapping is effective for emotional pain, and tapping in whatever manner you like is better than not tapping at all.

The method in which I demonstrate tapping is the way 99% of the tapping world taps. If you choose to tap in a different manner, do so. But please be aware that others around you may question the technique you use. To avoid the possible negative misconception of your method, have an answer ready for those who may inquire about details and your reasons why.

All stated, let me explain my vision for Christian Emotional Freedom Techniques. Let's begin with the differences between Clinical EFT used by non-Christians and Christian EFT. The differences are several-fold.

1. Christians believe it is God Who heals us. God the Father created us. He heals us at His pleasure and in the way He sees fit for each of us individu-

ally. "We are tenants or managers, not owners," states Malcolm Jeeves and R.J. Berry, using verses in Genesis 1:17 and Luke 12:42–48 to back up this concept.[8] Humans don't heal, except through the power of the Holy Spirit.

2. Christian EFT practitioners believe EFT is a tool of sanctification. Sanctification is a progressive process whereby we actively participate in clearing out and cleaning up our lives to be more in conformity to God's moral code as outlined in Scripture. That conformity and renewal of our mind come when we give our life to Jesus. At the time of our conversion, we are given the power to actively work toward becoming more like Jesus in order to give the world a witness as to Whom we belong and to Whom we give our allegiance.

3. To assist in the process of sanctification, Christian EFT practitioners employ confession and repentance within the tapping process. This moves us closer to a relationship with God as we confess to Him our faults, sins, and failings. Through repentance, we ask Him to help us break those habits and sins that disappoint and grieve Him. Sins are not just actions or behaviors. Our thoughts are just as deeply grieving to God as anything we sinfully do. EFT can be an effective tool to break down those sinful habits and thoughts, which separate us from our Heavenly Father. I repeat this quite often—much of our sinful behavior and thinking is something we learned from someone somewhere during our lifetime. Particularly as children, we watch and emulate behaviors we see adults around us do. Because children have no moral reference point, except for what adults tell them, children often repeat adult behaviors thinking them to be acceptable. The behaviors might be acceptable to another human, but God simply sees bad behavior in a different light and as one that is sinful. When we grow into maturity in Christ, allowing the Holy Spirit to point out our sinful behavior, tapping can be an effective tool in breaking down the thought and neuro processes that keep us trapped in those undesirable activities.

4. Christians understand the importance of prayer. For millennia, Christian believers have used prayer and meditation to ponder the great mysteries of God. Faithfully, we have spent endless hours communing with God, allowing the Holy Spirit to direct our lives in amazing ways. It is through this communication that we Christians seek God's wisdom for our lives

---

8   Jeeves and Berry, *Science, Life, and Christian Belief*, 221.

in the hope that we can in some way contribute to bringing the Kingdom of heaven here to earth while that path leads us to do works of charity for those around us. Prayer and meditation often go hand in hand.

Meditation is a wonderful tool to relax the body and bring stress levels under control. Dr. Joe Dispenza describes meditation this way:

"There are a lot of meditative techniques, but in this book, my wish is to help you produce the most desirable benefit of meditation—being able to access and enter the operating system of the subconscious mind so that you move away from simply being yourself and your thoughts, beliefs, actions, and emotions, to observing those things . . . and then once you're there, to subconsciously reprogramming your brain and body to a new mind."[9]

Rev. Clemons-Jones has these Christian thoughts on meditation:

"Some people have a hard time with the word 'meditate'. There have been many times that I have heard people say that to meditate is to be without thoughts and Christians should always have their thoughts on Jesus. Meditation is not thoughtless, and in fact, most of the early Christians relied on this discipline. Meditation is a reflection, rumination, thought, deliberation, and consideration. It simply means to mull over something and to look at it from different perspectives, to understand the various parts of it, and to weigh its meaning. It is to discover what God might be saying to us through a given passage."[10]

As a substitute for meditation, I use and teach EFT because this is exactly what tapping achieves. Both EFT and meditation accomplish similar things as indicated by Dr. Dispenza and Rev. Clemons-Jones. Tapping, like meditation, opens us up to changing our minds about our beliefs and our behaviors, giving us a mechanism to change both, bringing them into God's line of thinking.

In my previous books, I've talked about how stress works and why we need a technique like EFT or meditation to lower it. Briefly, I will again define *stress*: the higher our cortisol—and adrenaline, nor epinephrine, and other chemicals—levels within our bodies, all indicators of internal stress, the more likely we are

---

9   Dispenza, *Breaking the Habit of Being Yourself*, 176.
10 Clemons-Jones, *Cured But Not Healed*, 97.

to develop chronic illness. In his award-winning book *The Genie in Your Genes*, Church says:

> "But a recent study found receptor sites on the outside of cancer cells for adrenaline, indicating a straight-line biochemical link between stress and tumors. When we're stressed, our bodies are flooded with cortisol and adrenaline, and this study found that cancers grew 275% faster in stressed mice than in unstressed mice. The scientific consensus is that only 5% to 10% of cancer are hereditary; the rest are due to environmental factors, including stress."[11]

> As a side note, we often quote mice studies, "because humans and mice share a strikingly similar genetic blueprint – 99 percent of the genes in humans have a counterpart in mice – these studies provide us with a lens through which to view the effects of inherited stress in our own lives. This research is valuable for another reason: As a generation of mice is approximately twelve weeks, multigenerational studies can produce results in a relatively short time. A similar study conducted with humans could take as long as sixty years."[12]

Mice cannot tap, but we can, dropping our cortisol levels significantly.[13]

Like meditation, tapping drops our brain's wave states into alpha and theta wave states. I often tell my students that I don't have the desire or the time to learn to meditate well. I'm told by veteran meditators it is a skill that requires learning, and the more you meditate the better you become at it. Instead, I prefer to tap. If 2 to 5 minutes of thoughtful tapping—I'm paying attention to the tapping, not driving to the grocery store—will drop me into a quieter mindset of alpha brain waves, then I prefer to tap. We westerners tend not to take longer to accomplish a task than absolutely necessary!

Concentrated, intentional prayer is another form of meditation. Prayer works. Jesus taught us to pray. We are exhorted to pray often and pray with thanksgiving (1 Thessalonians 5:16–18; Luke 11:1–13; Philippians 4:6; Ephesians 6:18; Acts 2:42). Church again writes:

---

11 Church, Ph.D., *The Genie in Your Genes*, 255.
12 Wolynn, *It Didn't Start with You*, 35.
13 Church, D., Yount, G, & Brooks, A.J. "The effect of emotional freedom techniques on stress biochemistry," 891-896.

"Prayer has been the subject of hundreds of studies, most of which showed that patients who are prayed for get better faster.

One such study was done by Thomas Oxman and his colleagues at the University of Texas Medical School. It examined the effects of social support and spiritual practice on patients undergoing heart surgery. It found that those with large amounts of both factors exhibited a mortality rate *one-seventh* (author emphasis) of those who did not. Another was done at St. Luke's Medical Center in Chicago. It examined links between church attendance and physical health. The researchers found that patients who attended church regularly and had a strong faith practice were less likely to die and had stronger overall health."[14]

Based on those studies, why not combine prayer and tapping into our daily spiritual practice? Each in its own right appears to produce powerful effects on our physical, emotional, and spiritual health.

As Christian tappers, I exhort you to tap while you pray, and tap while you read your daily scriptural devotions. If lowering brain wave activity helps keep us healthy, then that in itself is well and good. But most of us Christian EFT Practitioners have found that while tapping in a prayerful manner, the Holy Spirit shows up in full force. There is something about quieting ourselves that opens us up to hearing the voice of God. While that may not necessarily be an audible voice—and there were times in history when anyone who claimed to actually hear the voice of God was deemed schizophrenic or delusional![15]—God can whisper ideas and thoughts in our thinking mind, which we all know is the Holy Spirit talking to us. Spontaneous thoughts can come out of the blue. Ideas that we know did not come from within ourselves because the ideas are out of character to us.

While tapping, particularly when we live with chronic stress, the blood flow improves to our pre-frontal cortex. When we are stressed, we often complain that we "can't think straight." There is a physiological reason for that inability to process thoughts. The blood literally drains from the pre-frontal cortex, where we analyze and plan our daily affairs. Prayer appears also to allow the blood to return to the brain where it is needed to function.

---

14 Church, Ph.D., *The Genie in Your Genes*, 67.
15 http://www.nytimes.com/2013/05/02/opinion/is-that-god-talking.html

God wants to communicate with us routinely. He likes for us to carry an ongoing minute-by-minute conversation with Him. He is our best Friend. We should be telling Him everything about our lives, thoughts, intentions, concerns, and gratefulness.

I highly suggest you routinely tap while praying. You don't need to do the formal EFT set-up and tapping rounds. Just pick your favorite tapping spot and tap on it. Tap on one particular spot, or pick a couple, and tap on those. Tapping complete rounds can be distracting to the prayer process. I'd stick to one specific acupuncture point, so you can tap without thinking about the actual tapping itself; therefore, you can concentrate on communing with the Holy Spirit.

Second, because tapping helps us think more clearly[16], I suggest you find a discreet way to tap during Bible study or during a church service while listening to the minister preach. Folding our hands during prayer is a long-standing tradition in Christianity. I boldly suggest we gently tap on the back of our prayer hand at gamut point while we pray. Since tapping takes us out of our stressed beta brain waves, relaxing us into an alpha space, what a wonderful way to allow God to unite with us in that prayerful time and place. I have often gotten wonderful insights from the Holy Spirit during sermons. He's connected more dots in my thinking pattern than I ever thought possible. He takes you deeper into His Word as you intentionally relax and listen to what is being taught.

Third, use tapping clandestinely to help you relax and quiet yourself when those around you begin irritating you. For example, while driving in a car with a friend who now has you trapped and insists on telling you every single thing that is wrong in her life, put your hand under your jacket and tap on the finger points. It will quiet your spirit and it will keep you from saying some comment you will certainly regret later. This tapping strategy also works in a business meeting or during an argument with your spouse or children. Let God de-stress you, so your anger and irritations are kept at bay. We are taught to simply walk away from disagreements. Sometimes, we can do that. Other times, we are so angry we don't, can't, or won't simply walk away. Teach yourself, mindfully, to start tapping at the literal second you feel any angst begin to rise within you. Stop satan in his tracks immediately. Truman states this best in her book *Feeling Buried Alive Never Die:* "The place to start is to become mindful or conscious of *what* you are feeling, *what* you are thinking, *what* you are saying, and *what* you are doing"[17] (emphasis author's).

---

16 Church, *The Genie in Your Genes*, 171-172.
17 Truman, *Feeling Buried Alive Never Die*, 87.

Tapping can help keep you under self-control the way Jesus Himself did. Self-control is one of the Fruits of the Holy Spirit. A Fruit we desire, but one that is difficult to cultivate. Allow God's reign in your life by tapping.

Fourth, in addition to prayer during our Christian devotions, we are instructed to add in Bible study and Scripture readings. We are reminded in 2 Timothy 3:16 that Scripture is good for "teaching, rebuking, correcting, and training in righteousness." Scripture encourages us, and it gives us God's own words as written by early Church fathers. Not only does the Bible teach us, it often also rebukes us by reminding us of what we are doing wrong. It instructs us specifically on what God requires of us to obey Him. His laws are for our own good. They keep us safe—not only morally, but physically and emotionally, too.

The Bible contains many verses on emotions. Jesus expressed His emotions. I suspect, anger is one emotion Jesus voiced when He overturned the money changers' tables in the temple (Matthew 21:12). Another emotion expressed is sorrow when Lazarus died. As Scripture tells us, "Jesus wept" (John 11:35).

King David's psalms are full of emotion—some emotions are cited in positive light and others in a negative manner.

Because Scripture is given for our training and correction, I have made a list of many of the more common emotions found in various verses. Some will calm us; others will instruct us to do better.

I recommend you choose some of these Bible verses, find ones that call to you, memorize them, and use them while tapping.

When I suddenly become filled with anxiousness, I personally find tapping to and reciting Philippians 4:4–7 helpful. I do so again and again until my spirit is reassured and my body calmed. Often, it takes just a few minutes for the Holy Spirit to rescue me from my own emotions.

Ronda R. Stone[18] at Heart to Heart Ministry in Oregon suggests a set-up and tapping rounds based on the following Philippians verse:

> "Do not be anxious about anything, but in every situation, by prayer and petition, with thanksgiving, present your requests to God. And the peace

---

18 2stones74@gmail.com

of God, which transcends all understanding, will guard your hearts and your minds in Christ Jesus." (Philippians 4:6)

"Set-up: Even though I am feeling fearful, I deeply love and trust in You. Even though I am feeling fearful and anxious, I deeply love and accept myself because You love me. Even though I am feeling fearful and anxious when your Word says not to, I know You love me and I love myself with that love too.

Tapping rounds: TH (top of the head) This fear. EB (eyebrow): This anxiety. SE (side of the eye): I am having trouble trusting in You. UE (under eye): This fear and anxiety is overriding my ability to trust. UN (under nose): This fear about_____. CH (chin): This anxiety about_____. CB (collarbone): I am full of fear and anxiety and yet, I want to trust in You, Lord. Show me the way to trust in You. UA (under arm): I release all this fear to you, Lord.

Round 2: TH: When I am afraid, I choose to put my trust in You. EB: Your peace transcends all my understanding. SE: I chose to have Your Peace and release fear. UE: I choose to receive Your Help. UN: You uphold me. CH: You promise to strengthen me. CB: When I am afraid, I know you are right beside me. UA: I put my trust in You because You are trustworthy and Love Me with an everlasting love."

Continue to tap, putting in your own words until the anxiousness and fear subside. At that point, feel free to tap your favorite Scriptures, thanking God for the blessing He just bestowed on you.

For the Christian EFT Practitioners, print out this following list and keep it handy while you tap with clients. Allow the Holy Spirit to lead you to a verse or two that He knows will impact the client on a spiritual level, assisting with whatever healing He is offering.

We all recite Scripture in our minds, so the biggest challenge to you would seem to be retraining yourself to tap while reciting. Remember, tapping doesn't have to be done overtly or ostentatiously. God put acupressure points on our fingertips, the back of our hand, and even on the outside of our thigh where the ends of our fingers touch the thigh while we stand. Tap or rub gently and slowly. Few people will understand or know what you are doing. Many people fidget, so friends will assume the same *anxiousness* in us.

As promised, please find below a list of general all-purpose healing verses. The list then advances to more specific verses for specific emotions. Use the verses freely as the Holy Spirit leads you. This is not, by any measure, an exhaustive list. It is simply a sampling of verses that you will hopefully find useful when tapping.

GENERAL VERSES

Philippians 4:19 And my God will meet all your needs according to the riches of his glory in Christ Jesus.

Isaiah 53:4–5 Surely he took up our pain and bore our suffering, yet we considered him punished by God, stricken by him, and afflicted. But he was pierced for our transgressions, he was crushed for our iniquities; the punishment that brought us peace was on him, and by his wounds we are healed.

Psalm 103:2–4 Praise the LORD, my soul, and forget not all his benefits—who forgives all your sins and heals all your diseases, who redeems your life from the pit and crowns you with love and compassion.

Matthew 6:33 But seek first his kingdom and his righteousness, and all these things will be given to you as well.

Psalm 41:3 The LORD sustains them on their sickbed and restores them from their bed of illness.

1 Corinthians 2:9 As it is written: "No eye has seen, no ear has heard, no mind has conceived what God has prepared for those who love Him."

Isaiah 58:8 Then your light will break forth like the dawn, and your healing will quickly appear; then your righteousness will go before you, and the glory of the LORD will be your rear guard.

Jeremiah 17:14 Heal me, LORD, and I will be healed; save me and I will be saved, for you are the one I praise.

Psalm 86:15 But you, Lord, are a compassionate and gracious God, slow to anger, abounding in love and faithfulness.

Romans 15:13 May the God of hope fill you with all joy and peace as you trust in him, so that you may overflow with hope by the power of the Holy Spirit.

Hosea 10:12 Sow for yourself righteousness, reap the fruit of unfailing love, and break up your unplowed ground: for it is time to seek the Lord, until He comes and showers righteousness on you.

Psalm 23:4 Even though I walk through the darkest valley, I will fear no evil, for you are with me; your rod and your staff, they comfort me.

2 Timothy 1:7 For the Spirit God gave us does not make us timid, but gives us power, love and self-discipline.

Psalm 31:19 How abundant are the good things that you have stored up for those who fear you, that you bestow in the sight of all, on those who take refuge in you.

Jeremiah 17:7–8 But blessed is the one who trusts in the Lord, whose confidence is in him. They will be like a tree planted by the water that sends out its roots by the stream. It does not fear when heat comes; its leaves are always green. It has no worries in a year of drought and never fails to bear fruit.

Psalm 138:7 Though I walk in the midst of trouble, you preserve my life. You stretch out your hand against the anger of my foes; with your right hand you save me.

Romans 12:2 Do not conform to the pattern of this world, but be transformed by the renewing of your mind. Then you will be able to test and approve what God's will is—his good, pleasing, and perfect will.

Zephaniah 3:15 The LORD has taken away your punishment, he has turned back your enemy. The LORD, the King of Israel, is with you; never again will you fear any harm.

Psalm 27:9 Do not hide your face from me, do not turn your servant away in anger; you have been my helper. Do not reject me or forsake me, God my Savior.

John 8:36 If the Son sets you free, you will be free indeed.

Galatians 1:10 Am I now trying to win the approval of men, or of God? Or am I trying to please men? If I were still trying to please men, I would not be a servant of Christ.

SHAME

1 John 3:19 This is how we know that we belong to the truth and how we set our hearts at rest in his presence.

Romans 6:16 Don't you know that when you offer yourselves to someone as obedient slaves, you are slaves of the one you obey—whether you are slaves to sin, which leads to death, or to obedience, which leads to righteousness?

1 Corinthians 6:19–20 Do you not know that your bodies are temples of the Holy Spirit, who is in you, whom you have received from God? You are not your own; you were bought at a price. Therefore honor God with your bodies.

Romans 8:5–6 Those who live according to the flesh have their minds set on what the flesh desires; but those who live in accordance with the Spirit have their minds set on what the Spirit desires. The mind governed by the flesh is death, but the mind governed by the Spirit is life and peace.

2 Timothy 1:12 That is why I am suffering as I am. Yet this is no cause for shame, because I know whom I have believed, and am convinced that he is able to guard what I have entrusted to him until that day.

Romans 7:24–25 What a wretched man I am! Who will rescue me from this body that is subject to death? Thanks be to God, who delivers me through Jesus Christ our Lord!

Acts 10:15 The voice spoke to him a second time, "Do not call anything impure that God has made clean."

Romans 6:21–23 What benefit did you reap at that time from the things you are now ashamed of? Those things result in death! But now that you have been set free from sin and have become slaves of God, the benefit you reap leads to holiness, and the result is eternal life. For the wages of sin is death, but the gift of God is eternal life in Christ Jesus our Lord.

1 John 3:9 No one who is born of God will continue to sin, because God's seed remains in them; they cannot go on sinning, because they have been born of God.

Proverbs 3:32 For the LORD detests the perverse but takes the upright into his confidence.

Romans 6:19 I am using an example from everyday life because of your human limitations. Just as you used to offer yourselves as slaves to impurity and to ever-increasing wickedness, so now offer yourselves as slaves to righteousness leading to holiness.

Proverbs 4:23–24 Above all else, guard your heart, for everything you do flows from it. Keep your mouth free of perversity; keep corrupt talk far from your lips.

Hebrews 10:22–23 let us draw near to God with a sincere heart and with the full assurance that faith brings, having our hearts sprinkled to cleanse us from a guilty conscience and having our bodies washed with pure water. Let us hold unswervingly to the hope we profess, for he who promised is faithful.

Colossians 3:1 Since, then, you have been raised with Christ, set your hearts on things above, where Christ is, seated at the right hand of God.

Philippians 4:8–9 Finally, brothers and sisters, whatever is true, whatever is noble, whatever is right, whatever is pure, whatever is lovely, whatever is admirable—if anything is excellent or praiseworthy—think about such things. Whatever you have learned or received or heard from me, or seen in me—put it into practice. And the God of peace will be with you.

FEAR

Isaiah 41:10 So do not fear, for I am with you; do not be dismayed, for I am your God. I will strengthen you and help you; I will uphold you with my righteous right hand.

Luke 8:50 Don't be afraid; just believe, and you will be healed.

Isaiah 43:1b Do not fear, for I have redeemed you; I have summoned you by name; you are mine.

Psalm 27:14 Wait for the LORD; be strong and take heart and wait for the LORD.

Matthew 14:27 Jesus immediately said to them, "Take courage! It is I. Don't be afraid."

Deuteronomy 31:8 The LORD himself goes before you and will be with you; he will never leave you nor forsake you. Do not be afraid; do not be discouraged.

Psalm 46:2 Therefore we will not fear, though the earth give way and the mountains fall into the heart of the sea.

Joshua 1:9 Have I not commanded you? Be strong and courageous. Do not be afraid; do not be discouraged, for the LORD your God will be with you wherever you go.

Psalm 34:17 When the righteous cry for help, the LORD hears and delivers them out of all their troubles.

Hebrews 4:16 Let us then approach God's throne of grace with confidence, so that we may receive mercy and find grace to help us in our time of need.

Psalm 56:3 When I am afraid, I put my trust in you.

Isaiah 41:13 For I am the Lord, your God, who takes hold of your right hand and says to you, Do not fear; I will help you.

Psalm 118:6 The Lord is with me; I will not be afraid. What can mere mortals do to me?

1 John 4:18 There is no fear in love. But perfect love drives out fear, because fear has to do with punishment. The one who fears is not made perfect in love.

Psalm 27:1 The Lord is my light and my salvation—whom shall I fear? The Lord is the stronghold of my life—of whom shall I be afraid?

Romans 8:15 The Spirit you received does not make you slaves, so that you live in fear again; rather, the Spirit you received brought about your adoption to sonship. And by him we cry, "Abba, Father."

Psalm 91:5 You will not fear the terror of night, nor the arrow that flies by day.

Matthew 10:29–31 Are not two sparrows sold for a penny? Yet not one of them will fall to the ground outside your Father's care. And even the very hairs of your head are all numbered. So don't be afraid; you are worth more than many sparrows.

Psalm 34:4 I sought the Lord, and he answered me; he delivered me from all my fears.

Hebrews 13:6 So we say with confidence, "The Lord is my helper; I will not be afraid. What can mere mortals do to me?"

Psalm 112:7 They will have no fear of bad news; their hearts are steadfast, trusting in the LORD.

Luke 12:32 Do not be afraid, little flock, for your Father has been pleased to give you the kingdom.

Psalm 3:6 I will not fear though tens of thousands assail me on every side.

Isaiah 41:13 For I am the LORD your God who takes hold of your right hand and says to you, Do not fear; I will help you.

HEARTBROKEN/GRIEF

John 16:20 Very truly I tell you, you will weep and mourn while the world rejoices. You will grieve, but your grief will turn to joy.

Psalm 147:3 He heals the brokenhearted and binds up their wounds.

Jeremiah 8:18 You who are my Comforter in sorrow, my heart is faint within me.

Revelation 21:4 He will wipe every tear from their eyes. There will be no more death' or mourning or crying or pain, for the old order of things has passed away.

I Peter 1:6 In all this you greatly rejoice, though now for a little while you may have had to suffer grief in all kinds of trials.

Psalms 40:1–3 I waited patiently for the LORD; he inclined to me and heard my cry. He drew me up from the pit of destruction, out of the miry bog, and set my feet upon a rock, making my steps secure. He put a new song in my mouth, a song of praise to our God. Many will see and fear, and put their trust in the LORD.

Isaiah 61:3 I will bestow on them a crown of beauty instead of ashes, the oil of joy instead of mourning, a garment of praise instead of a spirit of despair. They will be called the oaks of righteousness, a planting of the Lord for the display of His splendor.

Psalm 34:18 The LORD is close to the brokenhearted and saves those who are crushed in spirit.

Titus 1:2 [We live] in the hope of eternal life, which God, who does not lie, promised before the beginning of time.

Revelation 21:4 He will wipe every tear from their eyes. There will be no more death or mourning or crying or pain, for the old order of things has passed away

John 5:24 Very truly I tell you, whoever hears my word and believes him who sent me has eternal life and will not be judged but has crossed over from death to life.

Matthew 5:4 Blessed are those who mourn, for they will be comforted.

Romans 12:15 Rejoice with those who rejoice; mourn with those who mourn.

1 John 4:18 There is no fear in love. But perfect love drives out fear, because fear has to do with punishment. The one who fears is not made perfect in love.

Psalm 119:28 My soul is weary with sorrow; strengthen me according to your word.

1 Peter 4:19 So then, those who suffer according to God's will should commit themselves to their faithful Creator and continue to do good.

Psalm 88:9 ...my eyes are dim with grief. Call to you, LORD, every day; I spread out my hands to you.

Lamentations 3:32 Though he brings grief, he will show compassion, so great is his unfailing love.

REJECTION

Romans 8:16–17 The Spirit himself testifies with our spirit that we are God's children. Now if we are children, then we are heirs—heirs of God and co-heirs with Christ, if indeed we share in his sufferings in order that we may also share in his glory.

Galatians 4:28 Now you, brothers and sisters, like Isaac, are children of promise.

Psalm 27:10 Though my father and mother forsake me, the LORD will receive me.

Galatians 2: 20 I have been crucified with Christ and I no longer live, but Christ lives in me. The life I now live in the body, I live by faith in the Son of God, who loved me and gave himself for me.

Deuteronomy 31:6 Be strong and courageous. Do not be afraid or terrified because of them, for the LORD your God goes with you; he will never leave you nor forsake you.

Romans 8:1–2 Therefore, there is now no condemnation for those who are in Christ Jesus, because through Christ Jesus the law of the Spirit who gives life has set you free from the law of sin and death.

Jeremiah 30:17 "But I will restore you to health and heal your wounds," declares the Lord, "because you are called an outcast, Zion for whom no one cares."

Romans 8:39 Neither height nor depth, nor anything else in all creation, will be able to separate us form the love of God that is Christ Jesus our Lord.

Deuteronomy 23:5 However, the LORD your God would not listen to Balaam but turned the curse into a blessing for you, because the LORD your God loves you.

2 Corinthians 2:14–15 But thanks be to God, who always leads us as captives in Christ's triumphal procession and uses us to spread the aroma of the knowledge of him everywhere. For we are to God the pleasing aroma of Christ among those who are being saved and those who are perishing.

PAIN

Psalm 30:2 LORD my God, I called to you for help, and you healed me.

2 Corinthians 1:3–4 Blessed be the God and Father of our Lord Jesus Christ, the Father of mercies and God of all comfort, who comforts us in all our affliction, so that we may be able to comfort those who are in any affliction, with the comfort with which we ourselves are comforted by God.

Revelation 21:4 He will wipe away every tear from their eyes, and death shall be no more, neither than shall there be mourning, nor crying, nor pain anymore, for the former things have passed away.

Psalm 62:8 Trust in Him at all times, O people; pour out your hearts to Him, for God is our refuge.

REGRET

2 Corinthians 7:10 Godly sorrow brings repentance that leads to salvation and leaves no regret, but worldly sorrow brings death.

Psalm 37:3–6 Trust in the LORD and do good; dwell in the land and enjoy safe pasture. Delight yourself in the LORD and he will give you the desires of your heart. Commit your way to the LORD; trust in him and he will do this: He will make your righteousness shine like the dawn, the justice of your cause like the noonday sun.

Romans 8:1 There is now no condemnation for those who are in Christ Jesus.

2 Corinthians 7:9–10 …yet now I am happy, not because you were made sorry, but because your sorrow led you to repentance. For you became sorrowful as God intended and so were not harmed in any way by us. Godly sorrow brings repentance that leads to salvation and leaves no regret, but worldly sorrow brings death.

Psalm 16:8 I have set the Lord always before me. Because He is at my right hand, I will not be shaken.

DEPRESSION

Proverbs 17:22 A cheerful heart is good medicine, but a crushed spirit dries up the bones.

Romans 13:12 The night is nearly over; the day is almost here. So let us put aside the deeds of darkness and put on the armor of light.

Psalm 42:11 Why are you cast down, O my soul, and why are you in turmoil within me? Hope in God; for I shall again praise him, my salvation, and my God.

John 12:46 I have come into the world as a light, so that no one who believes in me should stay in darkness.

Psalm 62:5 Yes, my soul, find rest in God; my hope comes from him.

1 Peter 2:9 But you are a chosen people, a royal priesthood, a holy nation, God's special possession, that you may declare the praises of him who called you out of darkness into his wonderful light.

Isaiah 40:31 …but those who hope in the LORD will renew their strength. They will soar on wings like eagles; they will run and not grow weary, they will walk and not be faint.

Romans 5:3–5 Not only so, but we also glory in our sufferings, because we know that suffering produces perseverance; perseverance, character; and character, hope. And hope does not put us to shame, because God's love has been poured out into our hearts through the Holy Spirit, who has been given to us.

Psalm 28:1 To you, LORD, I call; you are my Rock, do not turn a deaf ear to me. For if you remain silent, I will be like those who go down to the pit.

Micah 7:8 Do not gloat over me, my enemy! Though I have fallen, I will rise. Though I sit in darkness, the LORD will be my light.

Romans 15:13 May the God of hope fill you with all joy and peace as you trust in him, so that you may overflow with hope by the power of the Holy Spirit.

Psalm 31:19 How abundant are the good things that you have stored up for those who fear you, that you bestow in the sight of all, on those who take refuge in you.

Romans 5:5 And hope does not put us to shame, because God's love has been poured out into our hearts through the Holy Spirit, who has been given to us.

Jeremiah 8:18 You who are my Comforter in sorrow, my heart is faint within me.

2 Corinthians 1:10 He has delivered us from such a deadly peril, and he will deliver us again. On him we have set our hope that he will continue to deliver us.

Proverbs 23:18 There is surely a future hope for you, and your hope will not be cut off.

1 John 2:8 Yet I am writing you a new command; its truth is seen in him and in you, because the darkness is passing and the true light is already shining.

Psalm 143:4 So my spirit grows faint within me; my heart within me is dismayed.

Deuteronomy 3:22 Do not be afraid; the LORD your God Himself will fight for you.

DESPAIR/DECEPTION

2 Corinthians 4:8 We are hard pressed on every side, but not crushed; perplexed, but not in despair.

Isaiah 61:3 I will bestow on them a crown of beauty instead of ashes, the oil of joy instead of mourning, a garment of praise instead of a spirit of despair. They will be called the oaks of righteousness, a planting of the Lord for the display of His splendor.

Romans 8:38–39 For I am sure that neither death nor life, nor angels nor rulers, nor things present nor things to come, nor powers, nor height nor depth, nor anything else in all creation, will be able to separate us from the love of God in Christ Jesus our Lord.

Psalm 31:5 Into your hands I commit my spirit; deliver me, LORD, my faithful God.

Romans 8:6 The mind of sinful man is death, but the mind is controlled by the Spirit is life and peace.

John 8:31b–32 Jesus said, "If you hold to my teaching, you are really my disciples. Then you will know the truth, and the truth will set you free."

Lamentations 3:21–23 Yet this I call to mind and therefore I have hope: Because of the LORD's great love we are not consumed, for his compassions never fail. They are new every morning; great is your faithfulness.

Psalm 13:1–3 How long, LORD? Will you forget me forever? How long will you hide your face from me? How long must I wrestle with my thoughts and day after day have sorrow in my heart? How long will my enemy triumph over me? Look on me and answer, LORD my God. Give light to my eyes, or I will sleep in death.

John 3:20–21 Everyone who does evil hates the light, and will not come into the light for fear that their deeds will be exposed. But whoever lives by the truth comes into the light, so that it may be seen plainly that what they have done has been done in the sight of God.

Psalm 42:5 Why, my soul, are you downcast? Why so disturbed within me? Put your hope in God, for I will yet praise him, my Savior and my God.

1 Corinthians 13:6 Love does not delight in evil but rejoices with the truth.

Psalm 29:25 Fear of man will prove to be a snare, but whoever trusts in the Lord is kept safe.

1 Peter 3:14 But even if you should suffer for what is right, you are blessed. "Do not fear their threats; do not be frightened."

Psalm 45:4 In your majesty ride forth victoriously in the cause of truth, humility, and justice; let your right hand achieve awesome deeds.

John 17:17 Sanctify them by the truth; your word is truth.

Psalm 116:3 The cords of death entangled me, the anguish of the grave came over me; I was overcome by distress and sorrow.

John 14:6 Jesus answered, "I am the way and the truth and the life. No one comes to the Father except through me."

Psalm 25:4–5 Show me your ways, LORD, teach me your paths. Guide me in your truth and teach me, for you are God my Savior, and my hope is in you all day long.

2 Corinthians 4:2 Rather, we have renounced secret and shameful ways; we do not use deception, nor do we distort the word of God. On the contrary, by setting forth the truth plainly we commend ourselves to everyone's conscience in the sight of God.

SADNESS

Jeremiah 8:18 You who are my Comforter in sorrow, my heart is faint within me.

Matthew 28:20 (Jesus said), "And surely I am with you always, to the very end of the age."

Romans 8:38–39 For I am sure that neither death nor life, nor angels nor rulers, nor things present nor things to come, nor powers, nor height nor depth, nor anything else in all creation, will be able to separate us from the love of God in Christ Jesus our Lord.

Psalm 37:4 Take delight in the LORD, and he will give you the desires of your heart.

Nehemiah 8:10b This day is holy to our Lord. Do not sorrow, for the joy of the LORD is your strength.

Psalm 55:22 Cast your cares on the LORD, and he will sustain you; he will never let the righteous be shaken.

Hebrews 6:19 We have this hope as an anchor for the soul, firm and secure. It enters the inner sanctuary behind the curtain.

Psalm 30:5 For his anger lasts only a moment, but his favor lasts a lifetime; weeping may stay for the night, but rejoicing comes in the morning.

Isaiah 62:5b As a bridegroom rejoices over his bride, so will You, my God, rejoice over me.

Psalm 13:2 How long must I wrestle with my thoughts and day after day have sorrow in my heart? How long will my enemy triumph over me?

Psalm 31:9 Be merciful to me, LORD, for I am in distress; my eyes grow weak with sorrow, my soul and body with grief.

OVERWHELM/TIRED

Matthew 11:28 Come to me, all you who are weary and burdened, and I will give you rest.

Psalm 34:18 The LORD is close to the brokenhearted and saves those who are crushed in spirit.

Philippians 4:8 Finally, brothers, whatever is true, whatever is honorable, whatever is just, whatever is pure, whatever is lovely, whatever is commendable, if there is any excellence, if there is anything worthy of praise, think about these things.

John 16:33 I have said these things to you, that in me you may have peace. In the world you will have tribulation. But take heart; I have overcome the world.

1 Corinthians 1:10a He has delivered us from such a deadly peril, and he will deliver us again. On him we have set our hope that he will continue to deliver us.

Proverbs 3:5–6 Trust in the Lord with all your heart and lean not on your own understanding; in all your ways submit to him, and he will make your paths straight.

Proverbs 16:3 Commit to the Lord whatever you do, and he will establish your plans.

Psalm 143:8 Let the morning bring me word of your unfailing love, for I have put my trust in you. Show me the way I should go, for to you I entrust my life.

Philippians 4:13 I can do all this through him who gives me strength.

Exodus 14:14 The Lord will fight for you; you need only to be still.

Psalm 59:16 But I will sing of your strength, in the morning I will sing of your love; for you are my fortress, my refuge in times of trouble.

I John 5:4 For everyone born of God overcomes the world. This is the victory that has overcome the world, even our faith.

Job 30:15 Terrors overwhelm me; my dignity is driven away as by the wind, my safety vanishes like a cloud.

2 Thessalonians 3:16a Now may the Lord of peace Himself give you peace at all times and in every way.

Isaiah 40:28 Do you not know? Have you not heard? The LORD is the everlasting God, the Creator of the ends of the earth. He will not grow tired or weary, and his understanding no one can fathom.

ANGER/RAGE

Ephesians 4:26 In your anger do not sin: Do not let the sun go down while you are still angry.

Exodus 34:6 The Lord, the Lord, the compassionate and gracious God, slow to anger, abounding in love and faithfulness.

Ephesians 4:31 Get rid of all bitterness, rage and anger, brawling and slander, along with every form of malice.

Proverbs 15:1 A gentle answer turns away wrath, but a harsh word stirs up anger.

Colossians 3:8 But now you must also rid yourselves of all such things as these: anger, rage, malice, slander, and filthy language from your lips.

Psalm 37:8 Refrain from anger and turn from wrath; do not fret—it leads only to evil.

Malachi 7:18 Who is a God like you, who pardons sin and forgives the transgression of the remnant of his inheritance? You do not stay angry forever but delight to show mercy.

Nahum 1:3 The Lord is slow to anger but great in power; the Lord will not leave the guilty unpunished. His way is in the whirlwind and the storm, and clouds are the dust of His feet.

Jeremiah 3:5 Will you always be angry? Will your wrath continue forever? This is how you talk, but you do all the evil you can.

Ecclesiastes 7:9 Do not be quickly provoked in your spirit, for anger resides in the lap of fools.

Proverbs 14:29 Whoever is patient has great understanding, but one who is quick-tempered displays folly.

James 1:19b–20 Everyone should be quick to listen, slow to speak and slow to become angry, because human anger does not produce the righteousness that God desires.

Proverbs 29:11 Fools give full vent to their rage, but the wise bring calm in the end.

Proverbs 16:32 Better a patient man than a warrior, a man who controls his temper than one who takes a city.

RESENTMENT/BITTERNESS

Ephesians 4:31 Get rid of all bitterness, rage and anger, brawling and slander, along with every form of malice.

Proverbs 15:18 The hot-tempered stir up dissension, but those who are patient calm a quarrel.

1 Peter 4:12–13 Beloved, do not be surprised at the fiery trial when it comes upon you to test you, as though something strange were happening to you. But rejoice insofar as you share Christ's sufferings, that you may also rejoice and be glad when his glory is revealed.

Psalm 145:18 The Lord is near to all who call on him, to all who call on him in truth.

Psalm 31:10 My life is consumed by anguish and my years by groaning; my strength fails because of my affliction, and my bones grow weak.

Psalm 71:20 Though you have made me see troubles, many and bitter, you will restore my life again; from the depths of the earth you will again bring me up.

Hebrews 12:15 See to it that no one falls short of the grace of God and that no bitter root grows up to cause trouble and defile many.

James 3:14 But if you harbor bitter envy and selfish ambition in your hearts, do not boast about it or deny the truth.

Job 5:2 Resentment kills a fool, and envy slays the simple.

Colossians 3:15 Let the peace of Christ rule in your hearts, since as members of one body you were called to peace. And be thankful.

Job 36:13 The godless in heart harbor resentment; even when he fetters them, they do not cry for help.

COVETOUSNESS

James 4:2 You desire but do not have, so you kill. You covet but you cannot get what you want, so you quarrel and fight. You do not have because you do not ask God.

1 Thessalonians 5:6 So then, let us not be like others, who are asleep, but let us be alert and self-controlled.

GOSSIP

Colossians 3:8 But now you must also rid yourselves of all such things as these: anger, rage, malice, slander, and filthy language from your lips.

Proverbs 11:13 A gossip betrays a confidence, but a trustworthy person keeps a secret.

Proverbs 18:8 The words of a gossip are like choice morsels; they go down to the inmost parts.

Proverbs 26:20 Without wood a fire goes out; without a gossip a quarrel dies down.

1 Peter 1:13 Therefore, prepare your minds for action; be self-controlled; set your hope fully on the grace to be given you when Jesus Christ is revealed.

Colossians 3:5–8 Put to death, therefore, whatever belongs to your earthly nature: sexual immorality, impurity, lust, evil desires and greed, which is idolatry. Because of these, the wrath of God is coming. You used to walk in these ways, in the life you once lived. But now you must also rid yourselves of all such things as these: anger, rage, malice, slander, and filthy language from your lips.

Ephesians 4:29 Do not let any unwholesome talk come out of your mouths, but only what is helpful for building others up according to their needs, that it may benefit those who listen.

DISCOURAGEMENT

Deuteronomy 31:8 The LORD himself goes before you and will be with you; he will never leave you nor forsake you. Do not be afraid; do not be discouraged.

Joshua 1:9 Have I not commanded you? Be strong and courageous. Do not be afraid; do not be discouraged, for the LORD your God will be with you wherever you go.

Romans 12:11 Never be lacking in zeal, but keep your spiritual fervor, serving the Lord.

Jeremiah 29:11–12 "For I know the plans I have for you," declares the LORD, "plans to prosper you and not to harm you, plans to give you hope and a future. Then you will call on me and come and pray to me, and I will listen to you."

1 Corinthians 15:58 Therefore, my dear brothers and sisters, stand firm. Let nothing move you. Always give yourselves fully to the work of the Lord, because you know that your labor in the Lord is not in vain.

Deuteronomy 32:10 In a desert land he found him, in a barren and howling waste. He shielded him and cared for him; he guarded him as the apple of his eye.

Ephesians 3:13 I ask you, therefore, not to be discouraged because of my sufferings for you, which are your glory.

Psalm 37:3–4 Trust in the LORD and do good; dwell in the land and enjoy safe pasture. Take delight in the LORD, and he will give you the desires of your heart.

Romans 8:24–25 For in this hope we were saved. But hope that is seen is no hope at all. Who hopes for what they already have? But if we hope for what we do not yet have, we wait for it patiently.

Matthew 6:26 Look at the birds of the air; they do not sow or reap or store away in barns, and yet your heavenly Father feeds them. Are you not much more valuable than they?

1 John 5:14 This is the confidence we have in approaching God: that if we ask anything according to his will, he hears us.

Isaiah 54:17 "No weapon forged against you will prevail, and you will refute every tongue that accuses you. This is the heritage of the servants of the Lord, and this is their vindication from me," declares the Lord.

Romans 8:31 What, then, shall we say in response to these things? If God is for us, who can be against us?

Psalm 143:9 Rescue me from my enemies, O Lord, for I hide myself in you.

ANXIETY/WORRY

Psalm 3:3 But you, O LORD, are a shield about me, my glory, and the lifter of my head.

1 Peter 5:6–7 Humble yourselves, therefore, under God's mighty hand, that he may lift you up in due time. Cast all your anxiety on him because he cares for you.

Psalm 46:10 Be still, and know that I am God; I will be exalted among the nations,

I will be exalted in the earth.

Hebrews 11:1 Now faith is confidence in what we hope for and assurance about what we do not see.

Isaiah 51:12 I, even I, am he who comforts you. Who are you that you fear mere mortals, human beings who are but grass…

Proverbs 3:25 Have no fear of sudden disaster or of the ruin that overtakes the wicked,

Philippians 4:19 And my God will meet all your needs according to the riches of his glory in Christ Jesus.

Psalm 38:9 All my longings lie open before you, Lord; my sighing is not hidden from you.

Philippians 4:6–7 Do not be anxious about anything, but in every situation, by prayer and petition, with thanksgiving, present your requests to God. And the peace of God, which transcends all understanding, will guard your hearts and your minds in Christ Jesus.

Matthew 6:25 Therefore I tell you, do not worry about your life, what you will eat or drink; or about your body, what you will wear. Is not life more than food, and the body more than clothes?

Matthew 6:34 Therefore do not worry about tomorrow, for tomorrow will worry about itself. Each day has enough trouble of its own.

Psalm 94:19 When anxiety was great within me, your consolation brought me joy.

John 14:1 Do not let your hearts be troubled. You believe in God; believe also in me.

Proverbs 12:25 Anxiety weighs down the heart, but a kind word cheers it up.

John 14:27 Peace I leave with you; my peace I give you. I do not give to you as the world gives. Do not let your hearts be troubled and do not be afraid.

Isaiah 21:4 My heart falters, fear makes me tremble; the twilight I longed for has become a horror to me.

Psalm 91:1–2 Whoever dwells in the shelter of the Most High will rest in the shadow of the Almighty. I will say of the Lord, "He is my refuge and my fortress, my God, in whom I trust."

James 1:6 But when you ask, you must believe and not doubt, because the one who doubts is like a wave of the sea, blown and tossed by the wind.

Psalm 121:3 He will not let your foot slip—He who watches over you will not slumber.

Psalm 18:10 The name of the Lord is a fortified tower; the righteous run to it and are safe.

Psalm 139:23–24 Search me, God, and know my heart; test me and know my anxious thoughts. See if there is any offensive way in me, and lead me in the way everlasting.

ABANDONMENT

1 John 5:14 This is the confidence we have in approaching God: that if we ask anything according to his will, he hears us.

Psalm 62:7 My salvation and my honor depend on God; He is my mighty rock, my refuge.

Psalm 119:114 You are my refuge and my shield; I have put my hope in your word.

Isaiah 54:7 For a brief moment I abandoned you, but with deep compassion I will bring you back.

2 Corinthians 4:9 …persecuted, but not abandoned; struck down, but not destroyed.

UNLOVED/SAFETY/INSECURITY

Psalm 18:35–36 You make your saving help my shield, and your right hand sustains me; your help has made me great. You provide a broad path for my feet, so that my ankles do not give way.

Lamentations 3:22–24 Because of the LORD's great love we are not consumed, for his compassions never fail. They are new every morning; great is your faithfulness. I say to myself, "The LORD is my portion; therefore I will wait for him."

Romans 5: 8 But God demonstrates his own love for us in this: While we were still sinners, Christ died for us.

Psalm 119:114 You are my refuge and my shield; I have put my hope in your word.

Hosea 14:4 I will heal their waywardness and love them freely, for my anger has turned away from them.

Job 30:15 Terrors overwhelm me; my dignity is driven away as by the wind, my safety vanishes like a cloud.

Jonah 4:2b I knew that you are a gracious and compassionate God, slow to anger, and abounding in love, a God who relents from sending calamity.

Jeremiah 31:3 I have loved you with an everlasting love; I have drawn you with loving-kindness.

Job 5:11 The lowly he sets on high, and those who mourn are lifted to safety.

1 John 3:1 See what great love the Father has lavished on us, that we should be called children of God! And that is what we are! The reason the world does not know us is that it did not know him.

Job 11:18 You will be secure, because there is hope; you will look about you and take your rest in safety.

John 14:21 Whoever has my commands and keeps them is the one who loves me. The one who loves me will be loved by my Father, and I too will love them and show myself to them.

Psalm 4:8 In peace I will lie down and sleep, for you alone, LORD, make me dwell in safety.

Nahum 1:7 The LORD is good, a refuge in times of trouble. He cares for those who trust in him.

Psalm 141:10 Let the wicked fall into their own nets, while I pass by in safety.

1 Peter 5:10 And the God of all grace, who called you to his eternal glory in Christ, after you have suffered a little while, will himself restore you and make you strong, firm, and steadfast.

Proverbs 3:23 Then you will go on your way in safety, and your foot will not stumble.

Galatians 2:20–21 I have been crucified with Christ and I no longer live, but Christ lives in me. The life I now live in the body, I live by faith in the Son of God, who loved me and gave himself for me. I do not set aside the grace of God, for if righteousness could be gained through the law, Christ died for nothing!

IMPATIENCE/PATIENCE

Proverbs 19:11 A person's wisdom yields patience; it is to one's glory to overlook an offense.

Proverbs 16:32 Better a patient person than a warrior, one with self-control than one who takes a city.

Ecclesiastes 7:8 The end of a matter is better than its beginning, and patience is better than pride.

Colossians 1:11 …being strengthened with all power according to his glorious might so that you may have great endurance and patience…

Romans 2:4 Or do you show contempt for the riches of his kindness, forbearance, and patience, not realizing that God's kindness is intended to lead you to repentance?

Hebrews 10:36 You need to persevere so that when you have done the will of God, you will receive what he has promised.

Colossians 3:12 Therefore, as God's chosen people, holy and dearly loved, clothe yourselves with compassion, kindness, humility, gentleness, and patience.

LUST/IMPURITY

2 Timothy 2:22 Flee the evil desires of youth and pursue righteousness, faith, love, and peace, along with those who call on the Lord out of a pure heart.

Colossians 3:5 Put to death, therefore, whatever belongs to your earthly nature: sexual immorality, impurity, lust, evil desires, and greed, which is idolatry.

1 John 2:16 For everything in the world—the lust of the flesh, the lust of the eyes, and the pride of life—comes not from the Father but from the world.

Proverbs 25:28 Like a city whose walls are broken down is a man who lacks self-control.

GUILT

Romans 4:7–8 Blessed are those whose transgressions are forgiven, whose sins are covered. Blessed is the one whose sin the Lord will never count against them.

2 Timothy 1:12 That is why I am suffering as I am. Yet this is no cause for shame, because I know whom I have believed, and am convinced that he is able to guard what I have entrusted to him until that day.

Acts 10:43 All the prophets testify about him that everyone who believes in him receives forgiveness of sins through his name.

Psalm 41:4 I said, "Have mercy on me, LORD; heal me, for I have sinned against you."

Revelation 3:19 Those whom I love I rebuke and discipline. So be earnest and repent.

1 Chronicles 21:8 I have sinned greatly by doing this. Now, I beg you, take away the guilt of your servant. I have done a very foolish thing.

Psalm 6:9 The LORD has heard my cry for mercy; the LORD accepts my prayer.

Ezra 9:6 I am too ashamed and disgraced, my God, to lift up my face to you, because our sins are higher than our heads and our guilt has reached to the heavens.

Acts 5:31 God exalted him to his own right hand as Prince and Savior that he might bring Israel to repentance and forgive their sins.

Psalm 32:5 Then I acknowledged my sin to you and did not cover up my iniquity. I said, "I will confess my transgressions to the LORD." And you forgave the guilt of my sin.

Ezra 9:15 LORD, the God of Israel, you are righteous! We are left this day as a remnant. Here we are before you in our guilt, though because of it not one of us can stand in your presence.

Romans 8:37 No, in all these things we are more than conquerors through him who loved us.

Psalm 7:3 LORD my God, if I have done this and there is guilt on my hands, forgive me.

Malachi 3:7b "…Return to me, and I will return to you," says the LORD Almighty.

Psalm 38:4 My guilt has overwhelmed me like a burden too heavy to bear.

Romans 2:4 Or do you show contempt for the riches of his kindness, forbearance, and patience, not realizing that God's kindness is intended to lead you to repentance?

Psalm 65:9 You, God, know my folly; my guilt is not hidden from you.

2 Timothy 2:13 …if we are faithless, he remains faithful, for He cannot disown himself.

Isaiah 6:7 With it he touched my mouth and said, "See, this has touched your lips; your guilt is taken away and your sin atoned for."

GENERATIONAL SINS

Jeremiah 14:20 We acknowledge our wickedness, LORD, and the guilt of our ancestors; we have indeed sinned against you.

Numbers 14:18 The LORD is slow to anger, abounding in love and forgiving sin and rebellion. Yet he does not leave the guilty unpunished; he punishes the children for the sin of the parents to the third and fourth generation.

Exodus 34:7 Maintaining love to thousands, and forgiving wickedness, rebellion, and sin. Yet he does not leave the guilty unpunished; he punishes the children and their children for the sin of the parents to the third and fourth generation.

PRIDE/HUMILITY

Proverbs 22:4 Humility is the fear of the LORD; its wages are riches and honor and life.

Luke 1:52 He has brought down rulers from their thrones but has lifted up the humble.

Psalm 10:4 In his pride the wicked man does not seek him; in all his thoughts there is no room for God.

Proverbs 11:2 When pride comes, then comes disgrace, but with humility comes wisdom.

Leviticus 26:19 I will break down your stubborn pride and make the sky above you like iron and the ground beneath you like bronze.

James 4:6 But he gives us more grace. That is why Scripture says: "God opposes the proud but shows favor to the humble."

Proverbs 29:23 Pride brings a person low, but the lowly in spirit gain honor.

Philippians 2:3 Do nothing out of selfish ambition or vain conceit. Rather, in humility value others above yourselves.

Proverbs 8:13 To fear the LORD is to hate evil; I hate pride and arrogance, evil behavior and perverse speech.

Luke 18:14b For everyone who exalts himself will be humbled, and he who humbles himself will be exalted.

Psalm 25:9 He guides the humble in what is right and teaches them his way.

Proverbs 15:33 Wisdom's instruction is to fear the LORD, and humility comes before honor.

Isaiah 2:17 The arrogance of man will be brought low and human pride humbled; the LORD alone will be exalted in that day.

Colossians 3:12 Therefore, as God's chosen people, holy, and dearly loved, clothe yourselves with compassion, kindness, humility, gentleness, and patience.

Deuteronomy 8:2 Remember how the LORD your God led you all the way in the wilderness these forty years, to humble and test you in order to know what was in your heart, whether or not you would keep his commands.

Isaiah 29:19 Once more the humble will rejoice in the LORD; the needy will rejoice in the Holy One of Israel.

James 3:13 Who is wise and understanding among you? Let them show it by their good life, by deeds done in the humility that comes from wisdom.

Proverbs 16:18 Pride goes before destruction, a haughty spirit before a fall.

1 Peter 5:6 Humble yourselves, therefore, under God's mighty hand, that he may lift you up in due time.

Daniel 4:37b And those who walk in pride he is able to humble.

Matthew 11:29 Take my yoke upon you and learn from me, for I am gentle and humble in heart, and you will find rest for your souls.

Psalm 147:6 The LORD sustains the humble but casts the wicked to the ground.

ENVY/JEALOUSY

James 3:14 But if you harbor bitter envy and selfish ambition in your hearts, do not boast about it or deny the truth.

Job 5:2 Resentment kills a fool, and envy slays the simple.

Proverbs 14:30 A heart at peace gives life to the body, but envy rots the bones.

1 Corinthians 13:4 Love is patient, love is kind. It does not envy, it does not boast, it is not proud.

1 Peter 2:1 Therefore, rid yourselves of all malice and all deceit, hypocrisy, envy, and slander of every kind.

UNFORGIVENESS

James 2:12–13 Speak and act as those who are going to be judged by the law that gives freedom, because judgment without mercy will be shown to anyone who has not been merciful. Mercy triumphs over judgment.

Colossians 3:13 Bear with each other and forgive whatever grievances you may have against one another. Forgive as the Lord forgave you.

2 Corinthians 2:7 Now instead, you ought to forgive and comfort him, so that he will not be overwhelmed by excessive sorrow.

Luke 7:47 Therefore, I tell you, her many sins have been forgiven—as her great love has shown. But whoever has been forgiven little loves little.

Proverbs 20:22 Do not say, "I'll pay you back for this wrong!" Wait for the LORD, and he will avenge you.

Matthew 7:1–2 Do not judge, or you too will be judged. For in the same way you judge others, you will be judged, and with the measure you use, it will be measured to you.

Mark 11:25 And when you stand praying, if you hold anything against anyone, forgive them, so that your Father in heaven may forgive you your sins.

1 Thessalonians 5:8 But since we belong to the day, let us be self-controlled, putting on faith and love as a breastplate, and the hope of salvation as a helmet.

Colossian 3:13 Bear with each other and forgive one another if any of you has a grievance against someone. Forgive as the Lord forgave you.

Matthew 18:21–22 Then Peter came to Jesus and asked, "Lord, how many times shall I forgive my brother or sister who sins against me? Up to seven times?" Jesus answered, "I tell you, not seven times, but seventy-seven times."

Hebrews 8:12 For I will forgive their wickedness and will remember their sins no more.

Galatians 5:22–23 But the fruit of the Spirit is love, joy, peace, forbearance, kindness, goodness, faithfulness, gentleness, and self-control. Against such things there is no law.

Matthew 6:15 But if you do not forgive others their sins, your Father will not forgive your sins.

Romans 2:1 You, therefore, have no excuse, you who pass judgment on someone else, for at whatever point you judge another, you are condemning yourself, because you who pass judgment do the same things.

CASE STUDY: KATHY – AN AVERAGE WOMAN'S STORY BY DEE WHITAKER LEGRAND

I met Kathy in one of my EFT women's group meetings and was impressed by her strong outward appearance and her great sense of humor. Kathy seemed confident, but I sensed her humor was diffusing her emotional pain. When I asked what brought her to my office, I saw a different side of her. She was full of regret about her past actions, dysfunctional family issues, work habits, failures in her marriage, weight gain, and her distance from God. She had a lot of intellectual knowledge about God from the Bible, but desperately wanted a relationship with Him, but didn't know where to start.

Raised in the Catholic Church, Kathy had a combination of extreme morality, dutifulness, and a hyper sense of responsibility—all of which resulted in her taking and enduring too much stress. She had a quiet sense of strength. Once her parents noticed it, they started giving her more responsibility with household chores and taking care of her siblings.

Her father was a raging alcoholic who was prone to drink and yell when he had one too many drinks. He too was loaded with emotional baggage from an abusive childhood, and he drank to numb the pain.

Kathy also felt her life was full of injustices, and she wanted to right the wrong. She perceived her early life as having been unfair, even abusive. She not only wanted justice for herself but for others as well. As she started a job at a law firm in college, the more injustice she saw at work, the quicker and more powerful her reaction to redress the situation. She excelled at the firm and had found that using her anger and passion for the underdog be-

came good fodder to set up her workaholic tendencies. She noted that being a workaholic was one of the few things in her life she was proud of.

After college, she succeeded at one corporate position after another and rose through the ranks quickly due to her ability to take charge and make change happen. Now, all the pressure that she put on herself to succeed had started to take its toll, and she had suffered from failing health and weight gain.

I explained to her what her body was really communicating to her when she released anger. God created our bodies to speak to us in different ways. Her symptoms were headaches, upset stomach, and neck or shoulder pain. Any of these symptoms may be a warning word from her body that a change is needed. I addressed the fact that she get in touch with those symptoms and start tapping on them and the feelings that they were producing as homework each week between our appointments.

In our next appointment, we delved deeper into her emotions. She started to recognize the anger that would wash over her. Often it had something to do with the current situation that brought back old emotional wounds, triggers, from her childhood. The hurt little Kathy was stuck and needed help.

As we tapped she learned that it was certainly easier and safer to rage with anger than to address the hurts and fears she had long felt. Her mother had become worn down from dealing with her husband's drunken rage and could not give Kathy the attention and love she deserved. Those memories, coupled with the pain and destruction of her marriage, had left her out of shape, unhealthy, and unhappy.

Some of the aspects we tapped on:

To be open to the possibility of self-awareness of her anger and stress. And receive clarity about her issue of judgments of herself and others.

That she was not alone, she needed to let the wall down around her heart and be open to asking for help. That she had a tool to use now whenever food cravings presented themselves to her instead of eating her emotions she could tap the cravings away.

We first tapped on releasing hurt and anger from her body because:

She felt trapped as a child because of the demands placed upon her and that she felt her childhood had been taken away, as she always had so much work to do that she never had any time just for fun.

The pressure she had put on herself because her parents were so dependent on her.

That she never felt that she was good enough at anything that she did because her parents never thanked her or even acknowledged her — they just expected her to do all the work.

We tapped in Scripture:

Lord I cast my anxiety and worry on you, because you care for me. 1 Peter 5:7

I know that I need not be anxious for anything, and I am thanking you for the work that you are doing in my heart. Philippians 4:6

FORGIVENESS

Through the tapping, she neutralized the hurt, and was able to forgive her immediate family. She also asked for God's forgiveness for her ungodly be-liefs, as we tapped on them one by one. We then went through the process of forgiving herself for all her critical self-talk, and for damaging her health by holding herself responsible for things well beyond her control.

She asked for God's forgiveness.

We tapped until she sensed that God was with her in that moment.

YOUNGER SELF

Several appointments later, she opened up telling me that she still felt vulner-able and frightened as she did often as a little girl. I told her that was a plea from the deepest part of her — the little girl that was still wounded.

We tapped on her healing by acknowledging and nurturing the needy child behind her negative feeling and thoughts instead of trying to push away her inner child needs.

As she learned to re-perceive negative feelings as pleas for attention from her inner child her life transformed into learning to realize more of the love of God had for her.

When we tapped on her inner child I suggested she ask:

What is the need behind my feeling, and what is it that my inner child needs right now?

As we worked together during our appointments she became much more aware of how she talked and treated herself since she was a child, when she felt anxious, lonely or angry.

She learned that she was healing much faster by acknowledging and nurturing the needy child behind her negative emotions instead of trying to push her away. By validating and loving her inner child, Kathy's self-esteem improved to the point that she was ready to tackle her weight problem.

WEIGHT LOSS

The next time I saw Kathy she had just picked up the results from her latest medical tests. She was still reeling from the report she received. She was 55 pounds overweight, her cortisol and adrenaline levels were much too high, her bone density was low, her immune system was suppressed, she had thyroid issues and her liver enzymes were elevated.

She was finally ready to lose her excess weight for the right reasons.

We tapped on:

Letting go of the need to bury her emotions with comfort food.

To stop binging when angry.

Releasing the chemical of anger from her body.

She gave herself permission to fully acknowledge her hurt, and her anger. To release the false story of her life that she developed from an angry and anxious little girl's perspective.

FATHER FIGURE

We addressed her father. She still felt terrified and humiliated from his loud ways and anger when he was drinking that frightened her whole family. Kathy was the one who always protected her siblings. She would shield them from any of his drunken moods and tyrannical outbursts. In some ways she still felt like that little girl that took care of everyone else, but there was never anyone to take care of her.

We tapped memory after memory of her dad drinking so heavily and becoming a belligerent drunk screaming and yelling. Kathy would shield her siblings from him, and tough it out herself. Often he would black out and not remember anything that happened the day before.

In our next session, she was dreading her dad visiting her. He was still drinking, very judgmental and opinionated, which made her feel as though she was still that little girl taking orders from him whenever she saw him.

As we tapped, anger washed over her. She realized that even though we had worked on dad before, there was another memory that came up of a time when a friend came over to spend the night and her dad was in a drunken rage by the end of the evening. Her mom did nothing to defend her from her dad, which made her feel ashamed and rejected by her mom. We continued with every memory of her dad until she felt no more emotion.

This took several sessions to completely neutralize all those emotions, as there were numerous instances that we needed to address.

Finally ready for the big day of meeting her dad for dinner, she took some deep breaths, tapped on the way to the restaurant and had her first authentic conversation where her own voice was strong and clear. She was no longer the little girl with the brave exterior who was trembling so badly inside that it made her want to go to the pantry to find comfort and safety in food. She was *learning to be secure in the knowledge that the younger Kathy – the one that was so wounded, was healing.*

CHRISTIAN COACHING WITH EFT

We started tapping on younger Kathy at Mass in church, and a disturbing image and memory came back of Father God. She realized that because of her earthly father, her image of a loving and compassionate God had been full of fear and shame. Her dad the dictator was how she had been referring to God her Heavenly Father.

We spent time in prayer as we tapped to open the eyes of her heart to see the truth about who her loving heavenly Father was.

TAPPING IN THE SCRIPTURES

We used the tapping to literally tap out the negative thoughts, beliefs, and traits that lie underneath the sins and fill up that space with the goodness of who God created her to be.

In Kathy's case – she wanted to tap with Scriptures that pertained to her sinful nature concerning anger, judgment, shame, and workaholic attitude.

Her tapping confessions were based on these Scriptures:

Luke 22:47–51 — Jesus response to such anger

Psalm 46:10 — An invitation to be still and know God and in this stillness to see the situation in its depth and fullness instead of making spontaneous judgments.

Luke 10:38–42 — The Martha and Mary scene was a good passage for her to tap on concerning her workaholic attitude.

Philippians 1:3–5 — Prayer of thanksgiving that she offered for the people that she felt deeply grateful for and who are loved by her.

Psalm 34 — This put her in touch with Gods justice and love and all for whom she felt compassion.

John 2:13–25 — This kept her in the presence of God where she now wants to live in the present moment.

Prayer and tapping became her daily morning routine.

GODS PURPOSE

Kathy was still starting to search for more meaning to her Christian spiritual life. She had recently found a church where she felt the Holy Spirit stir within her and fed her spirit. She knew that this was where God wanted her to bloom. Through her growth from the encouragement of the church, she filled out a spiritual gifts questionnaire.

Her spiritual gifts were that of a leader, someone with integrity that people would follow, and an advocate for the less fortunate.

PRAISE REPORT

I saw Kathy recently. She was well on her way to her weight goal. Her health had greatly improved. She was eating healthy, taking her prescribed supplements, and making time for herself each day. She was working on an average of 45 to 50 hours a week, and taking the weekends off. She was very excited about her next project where she would be heading up a church sponsored social justice outreach to the disadvantaged.

God is the God of second chances! Today was the day that she realized that she had found the God that she had been searching for. The inconsistency of her feelings and thoughts toward God was gone. She had always known that God loved her on an intellectual level, but today was the day that the gospel of grace had moved from her head to her heart.

Dee Whitaker LeGrand is a Believer who is a dedicated EFT practitioner and coach. She has worked with hundreds of Christian men, women, and children over the past decade in the area of restorative Christian EFT. She can be contacted at the following:

ChristianEFT@triad.rr.com
www.ChristianEFT.Info

CHAPTER 5

Christian Healing Visualizations

Once we have completed our negative emotional work effectively and efficiently, we can then begin to build positive-type experiences within our soul and spirit. These experiences must have two elements:

1. A visual of what we want for ourselves, based on God's will.

2. A positive feeling of what that picture looks like when we have achieved it.

We should focus on this in present time, not as something that will happen in the future, and it should be tapped and spoken of in the present tense.

Here are some visualizations that the Holy Spirit gave me. Try these techniques after tapping out the negative emotions. Sometimes we feel the need to fill up the space vacated by the negativity.

I BELONG/GOD LOVES ME VISUALIZATION FOR TAPPING

On occasion everyone feels alone, isolated, disconnected, and abandoned. For some of us, it is a lifetime feeling. No matter whom we have around us, or how many people are in the room, we never feel a part of anything or belong to anyone. It's a miserable feeling.

After you have tapped out all the negative emotions from any associated events surrounding the core issue of abandonment or loneliness, try this following technique:

Pick one of the face points and tap on it very gently, barely perceivable. It almost is a tickling feeling. Switch to another face point once you realize you must tap harder to actually feel it. However, keep this tapping extremely gentle. And I mean tap gently.

Close your eyes and picture yourself in heaven as you would like it to be one day, completely surrounded by all the millions of heavenly hosts, all of your dearly departed loved ones. And, most importantly, by God the Father Himself, seated in the middle of all these people surrounding Him.

Begin to pull from the core of your heart all that feeling of power and love that emanates from this immense host of saints and angels. They are rejoicing with you over your spiritual presence among them.

Picture people coming up to you by the droves, giving you hugs and patting you on the back. Every single person in heaven wants to welcome you home!

Feel the excitement of knowing this is what eternity will be like when your turn comes. As you gently continue to tap, add in any other details you want heaven to be, like huge food laden banquet tables filled with your favorite food, or beach scenes with endless white sand, or azure mountain ranges. Whatever nature scenes you enjoy, picture them in as much detail as you want. Feel into these scenes.

Keep up the light tapping and enjoy the moment for as long as you want, knowing you are part of the glorious host of saints living forever in eternity, in perfect peace and harmony.

As you hold that feeling in place, begin the floor to ceiling eye roll to integrate those feelings into your being.[19]

Something about this very light tapping evokes a different sensation within the body. Remember to go to this peaceful, joyful place anytime you want to feel loved and accepted. Use it during your prayer time, too.

---

19 See EFT for Christians Video # 9 for instructions on the floor to ceiling eye roll at https://www.youtube.com/watch?v=52GsyvzVJ1k&t=5s.

Do this visualization, along with all the positive feelings you can muster, for a minimum of twice a day to build up some positive, lovable neural bundles. It takes 21 days to change a thought habit. After 21 days, engage in this daily for a few weeks longer, and then as needed when you want to maintain the feeling. Use this imaginary place as your "go-to" spot of peace when life becomes stressful. Change details or even the location when you want. Such change will give you a variety of restful God places to think and feel into, giving you much-needed rest when times are challenging. Cultivate this peaceful place. Make it work for you to help calm you down.

We all strive for Philippians 4 "peace that passes all understanding," which Apostle Paul talks about in Scripture. This technique is a good start to help us get there.

GETHSEMANE VISUALIZATION FOR TAPPING

Rarely does anyone discuss the difference between the two emotions of shame and guilt.

EFT teaches us about two base emotions: fear and love. On the negative side, fear underpins everything; however, I hypothesize that shame, in many instances, is the big emotion directly below fear.

Shame covers many different angles of how we see ourselves. And because of these varying angles, each person who experiences shame takes that emotion into a different direction or behavior. Terry Wardle has this to say about shame,:

> Satan works hard to bind such individuals with deep feelings of hopelessness and an inability to change. The root of this lie is the stronghold of shame, a state of being that cripples and destroys.[20]

Shame is insidious, but, much of the time, we think we are "handling" it when, in reality, all we are doing is "controlling" it.

Controlling it means we are not resolving it; therefore, shame is still running our life from our subconscious level. We then put on a good act for others, trying to show we are dealing or have solved the underlying emotional problems of our shame. We lie to and tell ourselves that we really do feel good. We make statements like, "I know God loves me."

---

20 Wardle, *Wounded*, 132.

Consciously, our brain believes such facts, but as a wise pastor once said, "You must allow that belief to drop 18 inches to your heart."

If your heart and subconscious don't know or believe that you are loved, YOU won't emotionally believe it either. In reality, satan is keeping you trapped in the emotion of shame by telling you that you aren't good enough, you don't deserve anything, you feel damaged, you feel like a mistake, you feel unworthy and you live with no sense of belonging.

Once you have thoroughly worked through all the events relating to self-image and shame, try this technique:

Begin by tapping on your favorite tapping point or tapping without thinking about it on a comfortable point. Tap continuously throughout the visualization.

Picture yourself sitting with Jesus in the Garden of Gethsemane on Maundy (Holy) Thursday evening. All the apostles are propped against trees sound sleep. Do you hear them snoring?

Feel what you think Jesus felt. He is carrying all the guilt, fear, hatred, and shame of every person in the world who ever lived. It is beginning to build up for Him—all that pressure, knowing tomorrow Calvary awaits Him. Feel all that shame He is carrying for you.

Tune into where you feel it in your body. You may be feeling it absolutely everywhere. Shame is an overwhelming emotion.

Now, put a simple two-word name to your brand of shame. What would you label it? Your shame has a theme. What is that theme? Is it a sin you keep repeating or a habit you cannot break that shames you? A repeated statement or a name someone called you again and again? What exactly holds your shame in place?

Pick up a smooth rock you see lying near Jesus. Find another smaller sharply pointed rock nearby.

With the pointed rock, write your shame name on the flat rock.

Take a step back from Jesus. Watch His anguish as He wrestles with the sin of mankind. Look at His face. What does it look like? What is He thinking?

As He looks up at you standing there, thank Him for carrying all this pain for you. Tell Him how much you love Him for doing this for you. Hear Him tell you HOW much He loves you!

Walk over to Him and hand Him your smooth rock, the one on which you have written your shame name.

Watch Jesus as He reads what you have written.

Hear Him say to you, as He smiles an accepting, understanding, gentle smile, "Yes, it is mine to carry for you. I will take care of this tomorrow on Calvary."

Have Jesus say it to you as many times as you need to hear it.

Once again, tell Jesus thank you for dying on the Cross for you, then turn and walk out of that garden.

Jesus has your shame under His control; you no longer need to carry it. You are a child of the King of the Universe. You are loved unconditionally. Jesus did not reject your flat shame rock. He understood. He gladly took it away from you, so now you can be free to live for Him and to do His will as He has ordained for you to do.

IT IS FINISHED VISUALIZATION TAPPING

Often, we Christians simply can't seem to "let go and let God." This is probably true of most people in general, but I believe guilt drives many of us believers. We think we should know better, and we know we should act better. And we allow satan to continue to hammer us, even after we have confessed our sin to God, and we know He has forgiven us. Remember, the Holy Spirit convicts; satan condemns.

I often use this next technique at the end of a tapping session when a client has released a lot of suppressed emotions around an issue. After clients have confessed their sin that was tied up in a specific event, I use this "It is Finished" tapping technique to seal the deal.

This can be a difficult visualization to do if you are sensitive to thinking about Jesus' suffering and death, so please use this tapping technique judiciously.

Begin tapping on your favorite tapping spot and continue tapping throughout this visualization.

Close your eyes and visualize yourself approaching Calvary. It is Good Friday afternoon. As you walk along, Jesus comes into view, hanging in the middle of three crosses. His head is hung low; He is bleeding profusely, near death.

Gather up all the now neutralized tapped out emotions, events, and people and put them all into a container of your choice, such as a basket, box, or bucket. A small casket is appropriate here since these are now defunct emotional issues!

When you are ready, pick up your container and begin to approach the foot of Jesus' Cross. Look up into Jesus' dying eyes, and hear Him say to you, "It is finished. I died for issues like these and more. Leave them here for Me to deal with and move on to do My will."

Allow Jesus to repeat those, "It is finished" words as many times as you need to hear them, until you can set down that emotion container at the foot of the Cross.

If you are able, take note of the nails in Jesus' hands and feet and any other details around His dying. This is painful to watch, but know He did all this for you!

Once you have allowed the words of Jesus to penetrate your soul, and you can set down the burden of the container, turn away from Jesus, and walk back down Calvary's hill.

This last phrase tends to be the sticking point in this technique. Most clients are able to set the container down, but they cannot walk away from it because leaving that container symbolizes letting Jesus take care of our emotional baggage.

I've never had a client say, "I can't walk away from Jesus." They usually say, "This is hard. I can't leave the box there." Surrendering everything in our life is difficult, but this visualization gives us a chance to see ourselves actually doing it.

Continue to tap about walking away.

If you cannot walk away from your emotional container, you can approach this in one of several ways. You can redo this visualization as many times as needed until you *can* walk away. You can do a tapping round or two on the resistance of leaving that container at the foot of the Cross for Jesus to carry. You can apply the Floor to Ceiling Eye Roll technique. Or you can try any combination of any of these. I've never had a client who couldn't eventually walk away.

Usually, one of these techniques finally breaks the resistance, and you can walk away from the emotions, events, or people who once triggered them. I believe God uses this technique to loosen satan's condemnation hold on us. We no longer own the burden. It belongs to Jesus (Matthew 11:28–30).

NAIL IT TO THE CROSS TECHNIQUE

This technique is a softer version of "It is Finished"; however, you may find one is more effective than the other.

As always, tap continuously on your favorite tapping spot while doing this technique for the most effectiveness.

After you have neutralized all the emotions around a core issue, take a good memory or event that has many different sensory details in it, and use this visualization.

> Visualize yourself taking out a thick notebook filled with paper. Pick whatever size or color paper you want. Then choose a writing instrument—pen, pencil, crayon, marker, or chalk. In your mind, picture yourself writing down each person, aspect, or event from a tapping session on a separate piece of paper. Use one item or person per one sheet of paper only. Make this exercise sensory by seeing all kinds of bright or pastel colors, or hearing the sounds of crumpling paper, the scratching of a pencil as it writes, or smelling crayons, scented markers or pungent ink, even an ink bottle if you like calligraphy, or touching the texture of gritty chalk on your fingertips, or tasting the all-too-familiar woodiness of a pencil as you hold it by your teeth.

> Once you have finished writing out all the details on all those pieces of paper, picture in your mind the hill of Calvary with the three crosses on it. You might have hundreds of sheets of paper, or maybe only a half

dozen. Use as much paper as you want. Picture yourself writing down all the details of the memory you just tapped out.

When you are ready, gather up all those individual sheets of paper and begin to walk to the foot of the Cross.

This time the Cross is empty. Jesus is alive and has already risen from the dead. Only His Cross remains standing on Calvary.

Look at the foot of the Cross and see a heavy wooden mallet and a wooden box containing four-inch long hand-wrought square nails, three of which were used to nail Jesus to the Cross, lying there.

Pick up that hammer and nails and attach the handwritten papers to the Cross. Pound each one onto the Cross, individually. Take your time.

Read each paper to yourself as you hammer it onto the Cross. Do you feel any leftover emotions about any of the written items? If not, continue nailing the sheets of paper. If you do, make a mental note, or stop and write down the details of any unresolved issue. You should return to these unresolved items later and tap further on them to completely defuse those feelings.

Now, turn and walk away, leaving the papers gently flapping in the breeze.

Turn around one more time and look at the Cross.

This time notice that the emotion papers have all come loose and are blowing away with the wind.

Remember, Jesus has taken care of these emotions and events, along with any accompanied sins, which He has tossed as far as the east is from the west (Psalm 103:12). Those sins no longer exist in the mind of God.

You are now freed by the Cross of Christ!

EASTER MORNING VISUALIZATION TAPPING

This is a God-honoring way to use Christian visualization to "imprint" a godly image on the subconscious. It gives your thinking mind a boost toward allowing

God to deal with and handle the emotions that have held you captive most of your life.

Sit quietly after a tapping session and continue tapping on acupuncture points of your choice. This technique doesn't require any formal EFT.

> Picture a beautiful warm, sunny Easter morning just outside Jerusalem, and you are right there beside Jesus' empty tomb after both Marys found the tomb empty.

> The women have already discovered that Jesus has risen from the dead, and they are on their way back into Jerusalem to tell the other disciples.

> Stand there and stare at that empty tomb. Allow the colors and smells to penetrate into every cell of your body. The grave cloths are discarded on the inside slab where Jesus was laid late Good Friday afternoon. That huge round stone is rolled to one side. How could anyone move that? It weighs tons.

> Just like that tomb could not have contained Jesus' body forever, your subconscious mind cannot imprison your negative thoughts forever either!

> Now, picture taking a small broom and whisking out all of the "cobwebs" of emotions and negative thinking you have carried around for decades from all around you. God, through EFT, has knocked them all loose. Sweep them into your large dustpan. What color is the dustpan? How full is the dustpan?

> Look around you. Did you get all of those discarded emotions? Keep sweeping for as long as it is necessary to gather every one of them.

> Set your broom aside.

> Now, slowly enter Jesus' empty tomb, holding onto that dustpan tightly. Don't tip it! Duck, don't bang your head on the entryway.

> Slowly lift up Jesus' grave cloths and empty that dustpan beneath them. Shake it out, leaving every piece of dirt and emotion in that pile. Replace

CHANGE YOUR FEELINGS, CHANGE YOUR LIFE

the grave cloths as you found them, covering up all those sins, emotions, and feelings.

Can you see any of it anymore? No? So then, neither can God! He has tossed your sins and feelings as far as the east is from the west, and He remembers them no more.

Your memories may remain, but the perceptions around those feelings and events are hidden and safely stored away under Jesus' grave cloths. He is protecting them. You never again have to worry about them or deal with them.

Exit the grave and join the women and apostles who are rejoicing that their Savior is alive.

Thank Him for dying and rising from the dead to give you eternal life.

He is Risen! He is Risen, indeed. Hallelujah!

You are free!

ASCENSION VISUALIZATION TAPPING (FLOOR TO CEILING EYE ROLL)

This technique is an interesting Christian visual way to use the Floor to Ceiling Eye Roll.

Acts 1:9–12 reports Jesus' ascension into heaven from a Mount called Olivet, outside Jerusalem forty days after Jesus was resurrected.

Once you have finished tapping, envision the landscape of Israel—hot, dry, rocky, and mountainous.

Picture that Mount Olivet (or Mount of Olives), seeing the eleven apostles standing on that mountaintop with Jesus. This is where Jesus tells the apostles He is leaving the Holy Spirit here on earth with them to help them witness to the world Who He is.

Now, place your hand over your heart and begin tapping on your gamut point.

Close your eyes, and picture Jesus disappearing from sight as you and the apostles stand there watching. As He ascends into heaven from that mountain peak, roll your eyes from the floor to the ceiling.[21]

When using this floor to ceiling eye roll, stretch your eyes as far as they are able on both ends of the eye roll. This extra stretch helps to consolidate the neuro changes you just made during your tapping session, implanting them more solidly within both sides of your brain.

First, start your eyes at ground level where Jesus was just standing before He ascended and then roll your eyes heavenward. As your eyes roll upward toward heaven, envision Jesus taking all your pain and emotional angst to heaven with Him where He will safely store it away, never to bother you again.

Jesus is handling all the issues of life in His careful, concerned way just like He took them all on that cross at Calvary.

Repeat the technique as often as necessary, or whenever you want to feel and visualize Jesus taking away your pain, carrying it for you.

RELEASE AND LET GO TAPPING

This technique differs from others in that it is not a visualization technique. Use all of the statements that follow, or pick and choose the ones you feel the most connected to emotionally.

Our subconscious is designed to hang onto any thoughts or feelings for as long as it feels it is in your best interest to do so. It is a protection mechanism, so to speak. Because the subconscious mind is much more powerful than our conscious mind, we sometimes need to tell it what we want. I always do this "telling" while I tap. Remember, the tapping itself seems to open up that portal between the conscious and the subconscious mind. Anecdotally, we know it does release or open up a pathway because clients, while tapping, will remember thoughts, memories or events forgotten for decades.

---

21 See EFT for Christians Video # 9 for instructions on the floor to ceiling eye roll at https://www.youtube.com/watch?v=52GsyvzVJ1k&t=5s.

Again, I would not use this one until after I have done my negative tapping and confession to God. Clean out your emotional belief system before attempting to instill anything remotely positive.

As you use this technique, pay close attention to how you feel about each and every statement. Should any of the statements give you a physiological reaction, take note of which one, and later, during another tapping session, go explore the feeling. Ask the Holy Spirit what memory was triggered when you first said the statement. This might lead you to an entirely different line of emotional work God wants you to neutralize!

I've adapted this technique based on the work of Dr. Pat Carrington, professor of psychology at Princeton University. She called her EFT method the "Choices Method," whereby, we "choose" what we want, informing the subconscious mind of that choice. By adding Christian beliefs to this technique, it is one of the few times I believe using positive affirmations of any kind can possibly be appropriate while tapping. I strictly advocate keeping our tapping negative for the best results. But, occasionally, I find that clients want to try a technique that feels a bit more optimistic.

I let go of the unbelief of _____; I let in the Holy Spirit who indwells me.

I let go of the fear of _____; I let in God's faith and trust.

I let go of the doubt of _____; I let in the confidence of the Cross.

I let go of hurry and impatience of _____; I let in the poise and peace of Jesus.

I let go of hate of _____; I let in the love and forgiveness of the Trinity.

I let go of the folly and ignorance of _____; I let in God's wisdom and understanding.

I let go of the resentment of _____; I let in gratitude for blessings received.

I let go of the darkness of _____; I let in the freeing Light of Christ.

I let go of the gloom of _____; I let in the joy of my salvation.

I let go of the poverty of _____; I let in God's prosperity.

I let go of my weakness of _____; I let in the strength of Jesus' Resurrection.

I let go of my illness of _____; I let in God's vibrant, eternal health.

I let go of the discord of _____; I let in the harmony of the Holy Spirit.

I let go of the discontent of _____; I let in the serenity of the True Godhead.

I let go of all my tension of _____; I let in God's everlasting peace that passes all understanding.

I let go of the regret of _____; I let in the thankfulness of His loving hand.

I let go of the sadness of _____; I let in the joy of the Lord.

I let go of the guilt from _____; I let in the awesome forgiveness of Jesus.

I let go of the shame of _____; I let in the pride of being God's child.

I let go of the hurt from _____; I let in salve of the Holy Spirit.

I let go of the frustration of _____; I let in the confidence I have with His Word.

I let go of the anxiety of _____; I let in the trust of the Lord of Provision.

I let go of my lack of self-control of _____; I let in the stability of the Lord of Life.

I let go all my physical symptoms of _____; I let in God's mighty healing power.

I let go of the grief from _____; I let in God's overcoming peace.

I let go of the anger from _____; I let in the calmness of the Paraclete.

I let go of all the irritation of _____; I let in His soothing Grace.

I let go of all the emotions around _____; I let in the peace of Christ Jesus.

I let go of this inability to do _____; I let in a miracle that God can fix it.

I let go of my fears of _____; I let in the courage of being His child.

I let go of all my failure of _____; I let in the success He plans for me.

I let go of my feelings of overwhelm of _____; I let in the presence of God's angels.

I let go of all my disgust about _____; I let in God's acceptance and strength.

I let go of all my embarrassment about _____; I let in the pride I have in Jesus' love.

I let go of all of my self-loathing around _____; I let in God's encompassing love.

I let go of all my feelings of being disconnected from_____; I let in my connection to God.

I let go of all my sins of _____; I accept God's forgiveness.

I let go of my sense of worthlessness about _____; I let in feelings of being priceless to God.

I let go of all my insecurities around _____; I settle into the secure arms of Jesus.

I let go of all the feelings of disrespect about _____; I let in God's assurance of who I am to Him.

I let go of all the feelings of being unloved by _____; I let in God's everlasting love.

I let go of all the feelings of being unwanted by _____; I let in God's yearning to be with me.

I let go of the feelings of being used by _____; I let in God's servant attitude.

I let go of all the feelings of mistrust of _____; I let into my heart the faithfulness of my Savior.

DEE WHITAKER LEGRAND'S CASE STUDY: ANGELA THE WORRIER

One client, Angela, aged 48, was a constant worrier and full of anxiety. Even though she ate well and exercised, her long-term worry and anxiety had become extremely toxic. Her health conditions were numerous, including stiff joints, an autoimmune disease, thyroid dysfunction, and migraine headaches. She was also having tremors that would cause her body to shake and feel weak, most noticeably in her hands. All her energy was being spent dealing with her physical issues and her over reactive emotional state. She was easily triggered, and had been since childhood. Divorced from her husband, who had moved out of state, she was the primary caregiver of two teenage daughters. She worked part time, and most days her anxious worry would deplete her energy, so there was little left for her girls at the end of the day.

Her worry and anxiety had created a victim status. The best way to become a victim is to turn your mind into a place filled with self-hatred, unfair self-criticism, and gloomy predictions. Sadly, there is no place for God in victim status.

During our first session, she spoke about her feelings through tears welling up in her eyes. She had deep issues with conflict, and it made her uneasy bringing up memories of her childhood. She had grown up as the youngest in a family of four children, and the commotion had taken a toll on her. The commotion had affected her mom who raged with anger during which she would scream and yell throughout the day.

Early on, Angela felt her role was to be the peacemaker in the family. She was always putting her own hurt and emotion aside. She had buried them deep and knew that she needed help. A recent physical exam had revealed that her inflammation, cortisol, and adrenaline markers were greatly increased, and her arthritis had gotten worse. Her doctor had advised her to seek immediate help in dealing with her stressful emotional state. It was causing great physical discomfort as well as affecting her immune system. Her mental state of anxiety and anger was too much and was getting the best of her.

I asked, "What are some of the things you want most in your life?" Angela wanted harmony and unity with her family. As the youngest child, she had been picked on and bullied by her older brothers. Her mom had never intervened unless there was physical harm. She lived in a constant state of worry and fear, never knowing when one of her brothers would start the bullying again. In an effort to keep peace in the family, she began to avoid conflict by going along with everyone else and never letting her voice be heard. Since her environment was unpredictable, she kept a low profile so she wouldn't get picked on or blamed for something that she did not do. She felt she had to stay safe, and that meant not making any waves.

She had buried her deepest emotional hurts and felt like a victim to life's circumstances. She admitted she had never been authentic about her emotions. It was just too scary to confront members of her family. This led to avoiding conflict with her husband. She had been carrying residual anxiety and fear, and she felt cheated in life. She was now extremely angry about having denied the deepest part of herself—her God-given voice and strength.

Angela finally said, "I have been told that I am extremely sensitive all my life."

We talked about emotional triggers and where they came from in her life. She admitted a deep emotional trigger was her mom. She and her mom always triggered each other if they were together for more than a day or two. They were victims turning on each other.

Part of her really did want to heal and forgive her mom. She knew her physical condition was worsening, and her body was crying out for help. However, I quickly learned she had an inner conflict that did not want to budge. She wanted to continue to fume about her past and anything that came up on her unforgiveness radar—the misdeeds of her parents, her siblings, and her ex-husband. She saw it all through her judgmental filter of life. She was the victim, and even though she had spent a lot of money concerning her physical symptoms, and two of her physicians suggested that she get help with her anxiety and stress, she did not want to give up her right to judge both herself and others. She felt she had a right to feel that no one cared, and that God had dumped her into a cesspool of misery for the rest of her life.

She had never felt validated or respected by her mother, her brothers, or her ex-husband. She was easily triggered by each of them. And because she knew that one of the most harmful emotional triggers was her rage, it often came pouring out of her, with seemingly no way to stop it.

As I worked with her, she began to recognize the symptoms of the onset of her rage. I taught her she could deep breathe and immediately begin to tap. I assigned her daily homework in which she was to make a list first thing each morning of anything that she needed to address by tapping. She would also pray and tap in the morning to get the day off to a good start. She learned different ways to tap throughout the day. I suggested she tap one to two hours each day, so she could quickly create new neural pathways to a healthier way of thinking and feeling.

We worked on childhood issues. She was the baby of the family. Her mom was so busy with the other children that she didn't get much attention. The attention she did receive was always critical and angry. She realized she carried her mother's anger and critical voice. And, like her mom, she felt the world was not a safe place.

We tapped on:

"Even though I always thought worry was constructive in some way, worry is not a healthy emotion."

"I never learned how to express my anger because I had to deny it."

"I had a parent who often flew into a rage—no one modeled for me how to appropriately express my anger."

"Anger was scary to me, so I never showed it. Now I don't know how to control myself when I am angry."

After our first session, she felt much lighter and calmer. I suggested she set up a recorder app on her phone, so when she had a thought or an emotional trigger came up, she could easily speak it into the recorder and then tap on it when she could. We would go over her notes in each session, go through each trigger to see how she felt in her body, and note the emotional intensity. We would then clear the aspects of each memory one by one.

She noticed it made her day flow smoother when she took time in the morning before her children got up to add tapping with praying. Her energy was not drained as easily, and the fight-flight response was less noticeable as her anxiety and anger issues were not as close to the surface as before.

She told me that now when things were calm, it felt strange to her. She was accustomed to the rush of adrenaline and cortisol that her worry gave her. And when she did feel peace, it was as though a stranger was visiting her. Anytime she needed a rush of adrenaline, she would pick one of the festering inner wounds and create drama around it.

We continued to tap on her worry, the memories where worry was involved, and how she was always able to find something to feel worried about.

In a later session, while tapping, a memory of having been locked in a closet by one of her brothers came up. Having a fear of the dark, she banged on the door and screamed to be let out. All she heard was her brothers laughing at her from the other side of the door. I then used "re-right your history with Jesus" technique as she continued to tap. I encouraged her to step into that memory and invite Jesus to be with her in the closet. As soon as Jesus appeared to her, the closet door opened and she was free. She stood next to her brother who had locked her in the closet, and I asked if there was anything she would like to say to her brother. There were tears in her eyes as she continued to tap. She said she would let Jesus handle the situation. She then saw Jesus go up to her brother and gently touch his face. This affected something very deep in Angela's heart. She then realized that her brother was acting out because he too was the product of a very critical mother and an emotionally distant father. Just like her, his emotional needs had not been met by her parents. We tapped and she released the unforgiveness about her brother.

Once she went through a forgiveness protocol of forgiving her mom, dad, and brothers, it was time for her to work on forgiving her ex-husband. I sensed much more was inside those limiting beliefs. One reason she stayed with her husband and nagged him was because her mother had done the same thing with Angela's father, and it worked. Her dad became worn down, and feeling very committed to his four children, he gave in and did as she wanted rather than face his wife's rage.

In another session, she was very quiet but fuming. She seemed very angry. "What is really going on?" I asked. She said she had just returned from a visit from her ex-husband. I asked if this would be a good time to use tapping to release some of the anger and frustration she was holding. Nothing was good enough, loving enough, or worthy enough for him as far as she was concerned. She had not yet learned how to stand up for herself, and she still carried the hopeless and helpless feelings of not being good enough. We tapped on her emotions and ungodly beliefs that stemmed from her childhood to release them.

When I asked her how she related to Father God, she just shook her head. Her dad was distant to her and did not step in when her mother had screamed or punished her, so she thought of God in a similar manner. Somehow, God seemed to help other people, but not her.

I then asked what benefit did worry hold for her. She looked startled when I asked her that question. She honestly did not know how to be any other way; she had worried for as long as she could remember. Her worry was on auto-pilot.

"Okay, I understand. But what generally happens when you do this?" I asked. After some thought, she hung her head and groaned. Her body and paralanguage (the groan) told me everything I needed to know. She had the habit of using the "what if" in worrying. It had become so ingrained that she knew no other way to think. It had become part of her coping mechanism, complete with the loop thinking of helpless anxiety.

In Angela's case, after a few sessions to remove some of the immediate fears and anger, she had an "aha" moment. We tapped as she searched how she was feeling. She realized her dysfunctional relationship with her dad had clouded the lens of how she treated her husband in her unhappy marriage. Coming from one lie after another, she had learned not to trust her husband, and not to feel loved, respected or validated. She realized she had put God in the same category. She had a deep inner lack of hope. Her inner voice was asking, "Where is God in all of this? I felt hopeless and helpless as a child, and still do. Why does God help others but not me?"

After pulling out the root cause of her free-floating anxiety about herself, her family, and the world, she started looking within for answers. The wounded little girl who never stood up for herself, who always wanted to do whatever she could to keep peace in the family, realized her inner critical voice had been speaking so loudly that it drowned out God's voice. She learned to honor the loving voice within, instead of giving power to the critical voice. In many ways, her critical voice sounded like her mother's voice—nagging, sharp, and shrill. Like a lightning bolt, she suddenly realized that in many ways, she had become just like her mother.

During our next session, I asked if she completely trusted Jesus. She thought for a moment and said, "I think it's something else."

"Yes, I know Jesus went to the Cross. That is a fact. But deep inside, many cannot accept that he went to the Cross for them; I am one of them. I think, in my case, it was from my parental upbringing and the traumatic treatment from my brothers that I did not receive what I needed."

In Angela's case, it was due to an emotionally absent father, a critical mother, and the terrifying treatment from her brothers.

We tapped and tapped about not being able to trust and some of the events that had caused that mistrust over the years. Then she saw it—the symbol of Jesus and His love and devotion to her. She pictured a big wooden cross. I asked her to focus on the cross as she continued to tap and to let me know when she was able to trust Jesus fully because of what He had done for her on that Cross.

I then led her through a tapping exercise in which she renounced all the lies about Jesus. She then let Jesus take those lies from her and replace them with His love and compassion for her. At that moment, the Holy Spirit urged me to say a re-dedication prayer with her to the new *Jesus—the One she had now found and Who was Lord over her life.*

Angela is now thriving. She laughs often and doesn't have the same worry mechanism she used to have. She sees life from a different perspective—from God's perspective. She now knows that unity with herself, her family, and God has come full circle. She is now truly awakening to deep healing. Christian EFT is now the first tool she pulls out of her toolkit to take care of her emotional state and physical well-being.

Dee Whitaker LeGrand
ChristianEFT@triad.rr.com
www.ChristianEFT.Info

CHAPTER 6

Prayer and Scripture and Tapping

I'm asked often how I use prayer during tapping. Using the combination of both is a personal choice, but I do have some definite preferences on the subject.

Sometimes, besides opening a client's tapping session with prayer, I also use prayer during the session itself. Other practitioners also close sessions with prayer. These choices often depend on the individual clients themselves. Some clients want to tap clinically, just the way EFT is practiced, complete with the set-up and the tapping rounds. Other clients are more open to broader experiences and will try my recommendations.

I've done sessions with clients that are, from start to finish, one long prayer. Should passersby hear us in these sessions, other than the actual tapping, they would assume we were having an old-fashioned Wednesday night prayer meeting in church. In "prayer tapping" sessions, I tend to let clients lead. It's their session. Often, it truly does sound like someone just praying. One minute the client will be crying in intercessory prayer while the next she will be praising and thanking God for blessings received. Occasionally, I will interrupt her if I hear something expressly emotional come up. At that point, I might take over temporarily if I feel led by the Holy Spirit to do so and tap some traditional rounds on some particular feeling. With traditional rounds completed, the client goes right back into prayer mode. On occasion, we do find something specific, a memory or event, that needs a bit more tapping attention, and we together take care of the issue. The more open we are to the Holy Spirit's leading during our sessions, the more successfully we clear the emotions and increase the amount of work done.

Prayer is personal. It is relational communication with our divine, almighty Father. I don't believe there is any right or wrong way to use it while working with EFT. I encourage all of you to try tapping while praying.

During your regular prayer time, simply add in tapping. When not conducting official EFT tapping rounds, pick one acupuncture point or use several. Whatever you feel led to do is correct for you. I often use my finger points only and, sometimes, just one—my pinky finger. I specifically use it for one reason: it is an acupressure point along the Triple Warmer (TW) and the 9 Gamut (9G). The TW is a meridian associated with several other meridians—gallbladder, pericardium, and small intestine. When it is balanced, according to Chinese medicine, it gives us a stable mind, kind-heartedness, and the emotion of joy! TW sedating through tapping helps let go of old habits because your TW holds your fight or flight response, including rage, anger, and resentment. When we are in constant fight or flight, our immune system gets impaired, exhausting the body and causing some chronic sicknesses, including adrenal fatigue. I tell students to find an acupuncture point they feel truly helps them. I found mine. When you find yours, use it routinely. There is a reason you picked it!

Tap continually while you pray. I hear people tell me they only use tapping when they feel upset about something. My best advice is to tap the entire time you pray. Don't stop. Keep going.

Make it an open, honest communication with your Lord. I often walk down a street tapping away, praying to God in my head. We just talk. What I find amazing is how often God really opens up for me different lines of thought if I tap while I converse with Him. He gives me ideas that I would normally never think, let alone consider. Much of my writing is composed while tapping and praying. While I tap, I begin talking to Him on a subject, and I will simply ask His opinion or question Him as to why something happens the way it does. Answers come.

Praying the Scriptures is another way to use tapping with prayer. I don't use this method as often as my conversational one, but I know this is very effective. Sometimes, people will "rewrite" their favorite Scripture passages into their own words, using it as their own unique verses during prayer. Rev. Kymberly Clemons-Jones, a certified Christian EFT Practitioner, has this to say on the subject: "Praying the Scriptures is a sure-fire way to pray the will of God."[22]

---

22 Clemons-Jones, *Cured but Not Healed*, 96.

Ask the Holy Spirit for specific Scriptures—ones that will help you heal emotionally. He will lead you to the ones best suited just for you. Recite these verses daily or maybe several times a day until God releases whatever it is that is bothering you. God knows our weaknesses and tendencies (Psalm 139:2; Matthew 10:30), but tap as you do the Scripture repeating.

Prayer and Scripture are a dynamic duo like Batman and Robin. I'm going to call prayer and Scripture the "vital duo" because both breathe life into us, keeping us alive for Christ and protecting us from satan's strongholds (2 Corinthians 10:4).

Remember, a "stronghold" is any attitude or thought in which we think and feel the problem to be bigger than God's solution, eating up our life's energy and rendering us ineffective for God. Frankly, that was my former life. Every problem looked bigger than God. Now I understand where that thinking originated. As a child, I grew up feeling extremely ineffective. I felt misunderstood. No one seemed to listen to a thing I had to say. And the answer from every adult around me was "No"—no matter the question or request.

My sisters and I laugh looking back at our childhood now. When we would begin to ask mom for a favor, she almost immediately said "No!" before the request was out of our mouths. We had barely formulated the words and the request was denied.

Apparently, I was on my own to do this thing called life. There was no help to be found anywhere, including no help from God. I had built up huge strongholds that God demolished with tapping. I needed to get back to relying on Him for answers to life's snags and hitches, instead of relying on myself.

We often give the problem—and our thoughts and perceptions around the problem—way too much power. Please, don't take this defensively because I do understand your thinking on this. Before I began tapping, it was mystifying to me as to how to change my thought processes. Nothing I did worked.

We also give satan too much power. He is a defeated being. We have the victory in Christ Jesus. Satan deceives us into thinking he is in charge of our viewpoints and feelings when, in reality, we have built those up biologically since childhood. Satan has nothing to do with them. It is through correcting our thinking that Jesus heals us, kicking satan to the curb. That's exactly where he belongs as the non-entity that he is, powerless and subjugated, under the Cross of Christ!

We wage war on a spiritual basis, not an earthly one, even though our minds tell us this is a mortal fight. This carnal battle keeps us from functioning in our best God-ordained way. Fix your mind on God's solutions to life, not satan's cunning ways (Hebrews 12:2).

Ephesians 6:17 commands us to "Take the helmet of salvation and the sword of the Spirit, which is the word of God." Jesus has accomplished the first half of that verse. Now you are to grab the sword of the Word and fill up your thoughts with the Holy Spirit's point of view of who you are in Christ and how God wants you to live your life in Him.

Previously, we had tried everything to talk ourselves out of our emotional doubts and perceptions. The Word gives us the Truth (John 14:6). Tapping pulls out the negative thoughts from our physiology, literally, and then allows God's perspective to settle into our very cells, protecting us from future attacks from the enemy.

Tapping instills God's ways into our heart and mind, thereby helping us to walk in righteousness. Righteousness is an effective tool against the wiles of satan.

As you clean up your life for Christ, keep tapping. We are never finished with our work of sanctification until we arrive at our reward in heaven. Only then do our labors cease. Because of the deviousness of satan, just when we think we have a problem licked, he will sneak back into our lives, attempting to once again drag us down into that mire of emotional pain.

Don't allow him to do that. You must employ daily tapping maintenance. This is where tapping during prayer becomes so extremely effective. It reinforces and keeps those neural changes you have made strong and built-up. Be careful not to fall backward, necessitating you to begin tackling these emotional issues once again. God delivers us and keeps us delivered (2 Corinthians 1:9–11). He has handed us a tool to accomplish this. Do not neglect your prayer time and tapping.

A word of caution: please don't go looking for spiritual issues to tap about. This gives satan a stronghold. Allow God to lead you there. We cannot change everything in our personalities all at once. This is sanctification. It is progressive. It is a lifetime of growth. It takes time. Be patient with yourself.

Why doesn't God set us free once and for all in an instant? I don't know the answer to that. We all know people who have been set free in a second. Someone prayed for them and God simply took the issue away. For the rest of us, God is teaching us something. He has a plan. You've had to carry these difficulties for a specific purpose. Maybe the reason is simply that He needs you to now learn EFT. That was what He did with me. I begged Him for decades to take away my emotional pain. I thought He wasn't listening. He was. In His timing, He gave me a gift. The gift of EFT that I now appreciate more than had He resolved my problems in an instant. The decades of pain have given me a perspective on life that nothing else has. In God's eyes, each of our lives is individual, special, and unique (Jeremiah 29:11–12). I now see others' pain in a way no one else can. God has given me a purpose, and He has a plan for me—He always has. It's just that I see it now. Through it all, I can now help others. It's something I had done most of my life, but now that work has a more concrete structure with God as my foreman.

Just be careful when talking with our brothers and sister in Christ about their pain and their problems. Don't begin to judge their motives or their commitment to heal.

Remember, God has each of us in a different place in life. We all heal in different ways at different times, and some people never heal at all. It truly is our choice. And, sometimes, our subconscious mind has us so tied up in our pain we find excuses for why we don't act to resolve our issues. We simply cannot see a way out or any solutions to our problems. Simply pray for those brethren; it's God's job to help them. The only person you can change and are responsible for changing is **you!**

Permit the Holy Spirit to lead you to other problem areas in your life—as tapping itself will often do. We talk about "peeling the onion" in EFT. One problem gets resolved and another problem layer lies underneath the previous one. This progression continues as one concern after another gets neutralized. Use tapping and prayer to peel away your spiritual onion. Allow the Holy Spirit to show you where you are letting God down spiritually. As you tap, ask Him to show you incidences and times when this originated. Tap those memories out. Watch your behavior change into something truly resembling Jesus' nature!

Scripture can be used as prayer during tapping as you quote back to God His promises to you. I will admit, some days, I do get a bit more insistent that He listen to Himself about exactly what He has promised, but I certainly won't advocate you do that. Much of this is my own personality!

When I feel down about life—perhaps I just had a conversation with a friend about her health or finances, or the phone doesn't stop ringing with one request after another, or I'm just tired and feeling crabby—I will simply begin tapping and whining to God about my day.

Years ago, I felt that being crabby was my personal right. People shouldn't be irritating me anyway. Don't they know better than to bother me with their problems? I have enough of my own! I would just let anyone within earshot have it if they pressured or bugged me. God has made it perfectly clear to me that this behavior is unacceptable. He has given me a tool that I use routinely to immediately stop my unruly behavior. I excuse myself and I go tap. At that moment, I usually just tap on whatever it is I am feeling—irritation, anger, disappointment, discouragement, anything my body tells me is causing my crabbiness. Tapping eliminates that feeling of being inconvenienced by another.

Once I tap it all out, I then shift to praising God, thanking Him that He allows me to shift emotional gears quickly. Here is where I tap and pray my favorite Scriptures. I also use this exercise, when I suddenly begin to worry about something. I tap, confess the worry, and then recite prayerfully my favorite verses about letting God handle my life and all its circumstances.

Email me at EFTforChristians@gmail.com and tell me how you uniquely tie together prayer, Scripture and tapping. I'd enjoy hearing your comments!

CHAPTER 7

Christian Surrogate Tapping

Surrogate is "a person appointed to act for another."[23] As a verb, add another person or name after the word—*surrogating*, for say, a loved one or "to put into place of another as a successor, substitute, or deputy; substitute for another."[24]

Therefore, in surrogate tapping for others, we put ourselves in their shoes—feeling what they are feeling or thinking about whatever their situations are that have led us to tap about on their behalf. It is a gift we offer to others with no strings attached. We cannot conduct surrogate tapping to change the mind of others, nor can we do reframing for them. We are offering only healing thoughts and/or prayers.

Surrogate tapping can be done with the recipient hundreds of miles away or together with us in the same room.

An example of surrogate tapping is to tap on behalf of your children. We all have those days when the kids aren't doing what we wish or need them to do. Often, children are simply misbehaving. Perhaps it is Christmastime, and the usual holiday excitement has set in. Tapping for your children to slow down, to settle down, and to enjoy the holidays might be appropriate as long as you personally aren't doing the tapping because the kids are driving you to the brink of your tolerance level. The tapping intention needs to be for *their* benefit not yours. If your children are sending your personal emotions into overdrive, you must tap for yourself about those emotions, not about their behavior. Frankly, settling yourself down quite often gives you a different perspective and, sometimes, novel ideas come to mind as to how to handle your children in a positive manner!

---

23 Dictionary.com
24 Ibid.

Another example is your child having a tough time in school, so go ahead and tap for them. Keep your tapping focused on how your child may be feeling about whatever situations are going on around them. You cannot, however, tap for your child on something like "I will get a better grade on my math test." Or, if your child simply is not cooperating with chores around the house, you cannot tap "I will clean my room when Mom tells me to do so." Tapping is not mind-control; it is prayer-like empathy for another. In both situations, you can tap on their feelings of frustration, anger or perhaps even tune into what is causing the willfulness on their part and tap about that. Tap on what lies below the emotional surface, not the obvious unwanted actions.

It is important you detach yourself from the outcome. Only God can change how another person feels or thinks. We are responsible for changing ourselves only. This is why tapping must be for the other person's highest good, not to benefit you in any way. Do this work empathetically with their feelings in mind, not yours.

When conducting surrogate tapping work, allow the Holy Spirit to lead you intuitively. Remember, the Holy Spirit is our intuition; it is one of the ways He guides us. Many times, our *gut reactions* are Him warning us that something is wrong or immoral in a situation in which we find ourselves. I believe He talks to us through our bodily sensations, including pain.

Get out of God's way by tapping on yourself first about whatever the situation may be, so you are ready, willing, and able to accept whatever the tapping outcome is. Remember, surrogate tapping is for another, not you. Tap objectively!

As a Christian, I pray while I implement surrogate tapping for another. I have several reasons for doing this. First and foremost, I probably wouldn't conduct surrogate tapping for anyone with whom I didn't have a personal connection; therefore, as I tap and pray for another, I want also to calm myself at the same time about what I am personally feeling for my friend or family member. This allows me to focus more on the other person than on how I am feeling about the person's situation. Secondly, because I do have a personal relationship with the other person, I want to keep my own thoughts and feelings out of the tapping and praying, focusing instead on what *the other person is* possibly feeling.

We have available several different ways to surrogate tap. You may find a combination of these methods works better for you.

First, begin quietly tapping on any acupuncture point. Focus your thoughts on the other person. Consider in your heart how he is thinking and feeling about the situation in which he now finds himself involved. This can be done with the person a long distance away, or this can be done with the person sitting in the room with you.

You can tap in first person or tap in third person. I often use first person because I find it easier to get into the emotional thought pattern I believe the person is feeling. If you tap third person, use the person's name, such as "Jimmy is feeling sad because his puppy just died." If I were tapping on this situation, I would focus on how Jimmy feels about losing his puppy and say, "I'm so sad Blackie died today." Allow yourself to feel the feelings Jimmy would be feeling in this situation. Acknowledge, like you do when tapping for yourself, where you feel the emotions in your body.

I would tap on all the various emotions Jimmy is feeling around the loss of his pet. Again, by tapping on yourself, you allow any personal feelings around the death of Blackie to dissipate, too, or maybe, if you had lost a pet in the past, the tapping may enable you to focus on Jimmy rather than focusing on your own loss. In this situation, you may even obtain some generalization effects—tapping about something else often releases similar events or emotions about an event in our life—by tapping for Jimmy, your own subconscious may empathize with your own personal loss.

You can surrogate tap as often as you like for as long as you like.

Occasionally, someone will ask if we must obtain permission to surrogate tap as one is required to do when using surrogate Reiki. Gary Craig has always maintained that surrogate tapping is like prayer. We typically don't ask the other person's permission to pray for him, so we shouldn't have to be granted permission to tap for him either.

When surrogate tapping with children, you can use the same technique I outlined above. In some instances, children don't like to be tapped on. In other instances, kids like having another tap directly on them. If a child dislikes being tapped on, then surrogate tapping may be the ticket you need.

I know grandmothers who simply begin tapping on themselves, in front of a child, when the child is misbehaving or is having an upsetting day. The often interesting effect is the child will simply settle down because their mirror neurons will kick in.[25] Mirror neurons, discovered in 1995, make up much of our neurological system. It has much to do with the Einstein-Podolsky-Rosen Paradox that Albert Einstein and research friends considered in 1935, which is tied to the idea of quantum entanglement. They are what I call "monkey see, monkey do" neurons. Mirror neurons give us our empathetic tendencies. Often, when one person in a room yawns, others around that person will also yawn. When one monkey eats a banana, the other monkeys also want a banana. It may answer the age old question of why when one toddler has a toy, another toddler wants the exact same toy at that exact same moment! All of this has to do with our mirror neurons.

I also have heard from other grandparents that, sometimes, when they do begin tapping on themselves, a child gets upset even more, thinking the grandparent is trying to control him or her. It does seem children will eventually come around to tapping, whether directly on them or in their presence, if we gently tell them it is for their good, and we do it because we love them.

If I was tapping for a child who was in the same room as I was, I may not necessarily think or say anything about the situation. I would simply allow God's created mirror neurons to do the work for me. The child seeing you tap will often simply settle down.

An example of surrogate tapping could be tapping with a sick friend in hospice. We can sit quietly at their bedside and either gently tap on their hand or whichever acupressure point we can conveniently reach, or we can tap on ourselves for their benefit, thinking whatever thoughts you believe they would be thinking if you were in their situation. If the person for whom you are surrogate tapping is in your physical presence, take your tapping cues from them.

Illustrations: If a toddler is having a tantrum, screaming out loud, you have all the cues you need to tap for him or her. The toddler has literally just told you what he or she is frustrated or angry about. Use the toddler's own words for him or her, as you tap for that toddler—or use no words at all. It is your choice. If a sick friend has a high fever and is muttering some odd delusional sounds, tap about how your friend must feel right now and how he or she may feel upon awakening, wondering what he or she may have said that could potentially be embarrassing. We all see emotion in one another's faces, so watch and tap accordingly.

---

25 Church, *The Genie in Your Genes*, 200–203.

When we are led to pray for someone, and we know about the circumstances surrounding the prayer request, simply pray and tap what was said in the conversation that led up to that request. I estimate you have plenty of tapping and praying details to get started. Then lean on the Holy Spirit to fill in any missing details as they come into your mind. God knows what is going on, and He is faithfully listening.

You may use the set-up if you choose or just tap without the set-up. It's your personal choice based on what your comfort level is and your own general tapping procedures.

We know tapping is a calming exercise; therefore, using it in a troubling situation may be extremely beneficial. Since tapping drops a person's cortisol level (stress level), their DHEA level rises. As noted in my previous book, DHEA is a hormone produced by the adrenal gland to restore and renew cells in our body, allowing them to heal.

Touch itself is comforting to others. When touched or when we touch others, both parties receive a dollop of Oxytocin (OT), another hormone excreted by the pituitary gland, which simply makes us feel good. OT has often been referred to as the "love hormone" because of its bonding properties. It is an awesome hormone and, frankly, we can never get too much of it.

Surrogate prayer is also powerful. As a Christian, I equate it to surrogate tapping. Please allow me to relate the following story to you from Church's book *Genie in Your Genes* as an example of the power of surrogate prayer:

> ". . . the power of prayer across time comes from a study published in the *British Medical Journal* in 2001. In Israel, Professor Leonard Leibovici took a stack of hospital case histories and divided it into two random piles. The patients in these cases had all been admitted for blood poisoning. Names in one pile were prayed for, while the others were not.

> On later analysis, the group prayed for was found to have a reduced rate of fevers, shorter hospital stays, and a lower mortality rate. This kind of finding is typical of prayer studies and would not have surprised most researchers—except that the patients Leibovici *prayed for had been discharged from the hospital ten years earlier* (author's emphasis). The healing power of consciousness and intention appears to be independent of time

as well as space. Prayer seems to work retroactively as well as across great distances."[26]

In this story, no one was actually tapping. Instead, they were praying. This is what I personally feel surrogate tapping is—it is prayer. In the end, does it really matter which of the two methods works best? I don't think so. Prayer and tapping can be offered as an intentional gift to others for positive outcomes for them.

After reading this story, I was reminded that even though I may forget until days later to pray for someone whom I promised to pray for, it's never too late. Maybe intention alone is its own prayer. We do serve an amazing God, don't we?

Following are three more examples of surrogate tapping.

The first story came to me from a friend. Katie was taking an overnight airplane trip to Europe. Once she was seated, a child across the row from her began to fuss. Katie's thoughts, of course, were something like, "Oh, no. If this child cries all night, this is going to be a long trip!" So, knowing EFT, Katie began to surrogate tap for the little one. What did she tap? All the things she thought an 18-month-old taking her first airplane ride at night might think:

"I'm tired and I want my own bed!"
"I'm hungry!"
"Where's my bunny?"
"Why is it so dark in here?"
"Where are we going?"
"What are all these people doing here?"

And on and on she went with statements in her head, tapping away as she thought about them. It didn't take too long before the child quieted down and went to sleep, ending the plane trip from hell in fine fashion!

The second story I have used various times because of its importance. I'm in the grocery store when I hear a child begin to cry. Sometimes, the cry indicates a newborn, other times, it is quite obviously a toddler not getting his or her own way. I simply begin surrogate tapping by gently rapping my thumbs on the push bar of the grocery cart. I say to myself anything I think that child, based on my sight-unseen estimate of age, might be thinking:

---

26 Church, *The Genie in Your Genes*, 208.

"I'm tired and Mom is talking too much!"

"I wanted that candy!"

"I want out of this cart!"

"Can't we go home now?"

One hundred percent of the time with this technique, the child has stopped fussing within 30 seconds! One time, however, the child resumed crying again within a minute. I assumed it was the same child, so I started tapping once more and once again the crying ceased quickly. I never saw any of the children for whom I tapped. I heard them only. So how did this work? I don't know, but surrogate tapping, done prayerfully, settled down all the children!

The third story took place during a church service. The youngest daughter of friends I was sitting with began to fidget. My friend asked her to sit quietly on the pew beside her rather than on her lap. I could see where this fussing was going, so I began to tap on my gamut point on the back of my hand. It took a wee bit longer than my previous grocery store episodes. But, within 60–90 seconds, the child looked me square in the eye, stared at me for another 20 seconds like she was mesmerized, holding my eye contact, shrugged, turned and sat down on the pew quietly for the rest of the church service. Frankly, I was astounded at the time. What in the world just happened? It was a dramatic behavioral change for that little one who, in my mind's eye, I could see prior to my tapping being hauled out, literally, over her father's shoulder as she screamed and hollered, fighting the entire trip up the aisle and out the sanctuary door! I knew this child fairly well if you couldn't tell!

Do I use surrogate tapping often? No, not really. I usually tap while I pray for whomever I'm led to pray for. Frankly, the only reason I know it works is because I have tried it and it worked, as you can see from my personal examples.

Because I'm often asked about surrogate tapping and because I find it more like intercessory prayer, I wrote a prayer tapping technique based on that principle. I call this technique "Intercessory Tapping." I include it in the following subsection for your use. I hope you find it useful and invite you to teach others to use it, too. I also invite you to watch my YouTube Video on Surrogate Tapping.[27]

---

27 EFT for Christians Video # 25, https://www.youtube.com/watch?v=avPTqYS3oYo.

INTERCESSORY TAPPING

This technique seems straight-forward on the surface, but there is another dimension to it.

In Christianity today, we see the erroneous idea that those who are "intercessors" are called by God to a specific ministry. Scripture makes it clear that all Christians are called to be intercessors. We all have the Holy Spirit in our heart. And just as the Spirit intercedes for us according to God's will (Romans 8:26–27), we are all called to intercede for others.

Examples of intercessory prayer include Acts 12:5, Romans 15:30, Philippians 1:19, Job 42:8, Matthew 5:44, and 1 Timothy 2:1. And as Matthew 7:7 and Luke 11:9 state, it is our privilege as Believers to be active in intercessory prayer as God tells us to ask and it shall be given to us.

When the Holy Spirit leads us to pray for another—to intercede—I suggest we tap as we pray. Pick our favorite tapping spot and just tap along with our prayers.

Here is the reasoning for doing so: Intercessory prayer, at times, can become extremely intense. When we pray for our loved ones, someone close to us, we tend to have specific feelings around whatever the problem is. In other words, we feel the emotion somewhere within our bodies, and those emotions could well be negative.

What is the rule in EFT? If we feel a negative physiological reaction, tap!

When we pray for our sick grandchild, for example, I guarantee you that we have negative feelings around that issue!

As we offer a prayer to our Father in heaven, and we tap while doing so, we are also clearing out our own intensity around the issue.

What does this accomplish? It returns the 70% of the blood that has left our pre-frontal cortex back into our brain, allowing us now to be part of God's solution to the problem, not part of the problem.[28] We can witness to everyone involved that we truly believe God has it all under

---

28 Virkler Kayembe and Rice Smith, *EFT for Christians*, 131.

control by our actions. We quiet down our spirit, allowing God free reign to deal with the problem.

As we relax with tapping, the Holy Spirit will give us specific ideas of how we can help to alleviate circumstances around the problem, perhaps giving us a concrete way to help the family or the person himself with an act of kindness.

Not only are we bombarding the throne of God by asking for help and by showing others we trust Him, He gives us real concrete ideas of how to help others.

And we do "service" to ourselves as we relieve the past emotional pull we may have internalized about a similar event in our own lives.

I believe that as we relax with tapping and tune into what the Holy Spirit is saying, we also get more specific in our prayers, asking very intense and very detailed requests.

God is listening. And we are listening to God. So always thank Him for answering our prayers!

As I've mentioned previously, as a Christian, I believe surrogate tapping is another form of intercessory prayer. We often pray intensely for others around us. If we are willing to pray and tap, then we can simply add another layer to that process by acknowledging to God what the recipient of our tapping may be feeling or thinking.

Remember these finer tips about surrogate tapping:

- Do it prayerfully.
- Do it respectfully for the higher good of the other person.
- Allow God to do the work through you via the intercession of the Holy Spirit.
- You can surrogate tap for someone a continent away or for someone sitting in the same room as you sit.
- You can tap for others or you can tap on them, speaking or thinking for them how you believe they feel about whatever is going on in their life that needs some help from God.
- Do not be attached to the outcome.

- If you feel you want to change something about the person for whom you are tapping, do your own emotional work around the person and situation first before you tap for that person.
- Tap empathetically.
- Give God the praise and thanksgiving for the miracles He has already done in this situation – pray the solution!

In the final analysis, combine intercessory prayer with surrogate tapping. I believe this is yet another powerful combination that God has given us to help us heal and for us to help others heal.

CHAPTER 8

How to Begin Tapping

HOW TO GET STARTED TAPPING

I've had beginning "tappers" tell me they have read my two *EFT for Christians* books and now are so overwhelmed they have no idea where to begin.

Do you remember how you felt soon after your conversion to Jesus when more mature Christians told you to begin reading the Scriptures? What did you do? If you hadn't yet been given a Bible, you went out and purchased one after, hopefully, asking for opinions about which version to buy. You thumbed through it completely overwhelmed by where to begin that 1200-page tome. So how did you actually start? You picked up the book and began reading it. Perhaps you had a specific plan or maybe you didn't.

Tapping is no different. Start tapping. Use what you remember from your reading and begin practicing. The beauty of EFT for beginners is that you can do no harm to yourself simply by tapping acupuncture points.

Let God figure out where He wants you to go emotionally with the tapping. Don't be too hard on yourself. Learning EFT is no different than learning any other skill. Seriously, there is no difference here. Keep in mind that all now-seasoned tappers were once beginners, too. God dropped the idea of EFT on us; we responded to His gentle admonition and began using the technique. Did we flub up when we first started? You bet we did! Did we feel overwhelmed trying to remember all the steps and points? I found it all frustrating. We always want to do a newly learned thing perfectly the first time we try it.

Most often we aren't too successful. Don't panic. Don't quit. Don't allow satan to overwhelm you. He's not interested in seeing you healed. Don't give into the temptation to stop. Persevere and keep trying!

Here's my best advice to all new EFT "tappers".

Read through the how-to Emotional Freedom Techniques manual found in the first *EFT for Christians* book. It is about 64 pages long. Read it a couple of times. Let some of the nuances begin to stick in your head. Be thoughtful about the reading, so don't watch television while you read.

If thumbing through the book is too cumbersome while you practice tapping, take a sheet or two of paper and write the technique out in steps in a manner you can easily follow for yourself. I did this myself. I wrote myself an introductory how-to tap sheet. The simple act of writing down the steps helps imprint more of the process in your memory.

Now, once the physical tapping process is written out, take some time every day just practicing how to tap. Learn the acupressure points first. Get that rhythm down, so you don't even have to think about it. Automatically when you start tapping, the sequence comes without thought, and you know you are tapping 5-9 times on each acupuncture point.

Remember, there is no "magic" to this number. You could probably tap an entire hour session on one point, and it would still be effective. The reason for the multiple points is each acupuncture point corresponds to a specific meridian that flows through specific body organs. We have found that certain organs seem to trap certain emotions. By tapping as many acupuncture points as possible during an EFT sessions, you may be clearing out emotions trapped in places you haven't yet discovered.

Remember, the set-up needs to be specific to you. Specificity is what gets the job done in tapping. Generalizations and global statements aren't helpful at all, and that is why I never recommend scripts and watching most YouTube videos, hoping to actually get relief. Watching and tapping to a YouTube video on anxiety will give you a wee bit of relief, but you will certainly get the bigger bang for your buck IF you learn how to tap very specifically on aspects (details) around your own anxiousness and what memories or events bolster it.

Now, begin to add in the verbiage. Go to the side of your hand (SOH) or karate chop point[29] (KC) and begin crafting your set-up statements.

Example: How best do you get a wall painted? Picking up the whole can of paint and throwing it at the wall? That will get some of the job done, but in the process making a great big mess, leaving most of the wall still untouched. The same is true with tapping. You can do a perfect set-up, tap correctly on each and every point, but if you are not feeling and thinking specifically about what is bothering you, you will only get limited results like the paint-splashed walls on which paint went everywhere except where you really wanted it to go!

Don't tap. . .

> "I feel bad."
> "I hate my job."
> "I can't get along with my wife."
> "My children won't listen."

. . . or other generalities like that and expect to obtain any tapping results. I can guarantee you will give up on tapping quickly because you will find it doesn't work.

This is why I don't advocate using YouTube video scripts. They can teach you tapping points, and maybe cadence, but learn how to get specific about emotional things in your own life if you really want amazing EFT results.

Create explicit problem statements to tap on and get specific by finding where in your body you feel that statement resides. Feel into your body. For some of us, this takes practice. Don't give up if you can't do this right away. Practice feeling your body. I guarantee the feeling is in that body of yours somewhere. When we have stuffed our concerns and passions for decades, trying not to feel them, it takes some time to restart the ability to feel again. Be patient, please.

Frankly, some of the problems in your life are because you CAN'T feel what your body is trying to tell you. The Holy Spirit often speaks to us via our bodily sensations. The Father gave us this body for more uses than getting from point A to point B every day. It's a storehouse of wonderful emotions, both good and bad.

---

29 Both certifying bodies -AAMET and EFTUniverse - have officially changed the "karate chop" point to the "side of the hand" point.

It's the bad ones that can eventually cause you physical illnesses. It's time to learn to let them go through a technique that quite often works well.

Now, get specific. How does that problem statement make your body feel? Is it angry, sad, anxious, resentful, regretful, or discouraged? Where precisely is the feeling? What area of the body? Is it in your stomach? Upper, lower, or mid-gut? Your throat? Your jaw? Describe the area with two or three adjectives.

Make it a rule to give whatever you are tapping about a two-to-three-adjectives description. This rule makes you get SPECIFIC about what you are feeling. As an old jingle proclaimed: "For results that are terrific, get specific!"

You're now on your way to learning to tap in a very precise and effective way.

Practice each step until you are comfortable and can perform the step without thinking. Learn to tap like a robot. Let the technique itself flow. Then all you must do is change up the emotional component each time you use EFT. Remember, be specific.

1. You have a known emotion.

2. You now know where the emotion lives in your body.

You have a few extra descriptive words about exactly what it feels like.

Now use all that to set-up your session.

1. Even though I have this feeling (insert your own)

2. And I feel it in (insert your body part)

3. And it feels like (insert your 2 or 3 adjectives)

4. Add your acceptance statement.

In both of my *EFT for Christians* books, I have given multiple examples of Christian EFT set-up statements. In regular Clinical EFT, the statement is this in its entirety:

"Even though I have this problem (insert the specifics as outlined above), I deeply and completely accept myself."

Some trainers will add in "love and accept myself," but Founder Gary Craig dropped the "love" part fairly quickly because he understood that many people didn't love themselves, so they couldn't make themselves say that statement.

The acceptance statement is just that—an acceptance statement. Whatever you want or need to insert in there that rings true to you is absolutely acceptable. Anything goes, literally. You can make that statement as positive as you want, or you can make a positive acceptance statement that adds something like:

"and I wish I really did feel this way, but I don't. Perhaps one day God will help me to really feel that way."

Or add any variation of any statement you feel is positive or comfortable for you. Feel free during the acceptance statement to quote Scripture or use one of your favorite prayers, crafting it into a personal acceptance statement.

Remember, EFT is very forgiving. It allows you to mess up, and it will often still work. Now, that statement doesn't give you license to fumble your way through the tapping technique because you refuse to take the time to learn to do it well. Anything in life worth learning, as the old adage says, is worth learning well. What I mean when I say EFT is forgiving is **for you to give yourself permission to go easy on yourself until you have comprehended the full and complete technique**. In this case, practice truly does make perfect. Everyone who today taps effectively for themselves or with others started right where you are now, flubbing and fumbling their way through tapping, thinking they would never get this technique right. Well, they did.

Now, for the next piece of the technique, you will need reminder statements to use while tapping on each individual acupressure point. What's a reminder statement? Short phrases from all the language you used to set-up this tapping session. Phrases that keep your mind sharply focused on exactly what you are tapping about. This is important so your mind doesn't wander off thinking about your grocery list, what time you must pick up the kids from school, or what it was your husband mumbled about needing you to do this weekend as he rushed out the front door to work while you were still half asleep.

A couple of specific impactful words will do it. Don't wander off onto another emotional path or memory. Stay focused right where you started. Finish off one memory or event before moving to the next. Take note of what else pops into your mind because your subconscious mind is already showing you the brightly lit next step.

When you sense the feeling lessen here, and you probably will only need 1-3 rounds of tapping, stop and re-evaluate yours SUDS (subjective units of distress) emotional number, which is similar to when a doctor asks you how much physical pain you are having on a scale of 0 to 10—0 SUDS is no emotional pain about an incident and a 10 SUDS means the feeling is horrific. As the name suggests, this is totally subjective, so there is no right or wrong answer. SUDS simply give you a mental idea of how well EFT is working throughout a session. In general, when we see something working well, we are encouraged to continue using it.

Just before you set up your tapping session, tune into the emotional discomfort and rate it from a 0 to 10 SUDS. Then after tapping for a couple of rounds, rate the emotional pain again. Is it down? Or is it up?

Both are fine, but in different ways. If it is down, continue doing a couple of rounds using the "remaining" language. Often, this will drop you quickly to a zero. When the SUDS hit a 3 or lower, I incorporate the "remaining" statement. It sounds like this:

"Even though I have this remaining _____, I know that God loves me so much that He sent Jesus to earth as an infant child to gain me a place in heaven," (or whatever acceptance statement you choose to insert here).

Tap two rounds and recheck SUDS. You will most likely find it to be at 0.

When the SUDS hit zero, tune back into the memory or event and do this process over again with another emotion until you have all the feeling pieces pulled out of that specific memory.

Next step is to start the process again with another memory or event. Do this again and again until you begin to feel calmer and more controlled in life. It is progressive. It often takes time. God often heals slowly. Your body needs to heal from all the stress you have subjected it over the past several decades. You may get instant relief on some levels. But remember, you didn't get into this emotionally negative boat overnight, so most likely you won't exit it overnight either! Be patient with EFT and be patient with yourself.

If the SUDS elevate with tapping instead of decreasing, don't panic. It's a sign to you that your subconscious mind has simply tapped into another memory that might well have more emotion packed into it than the memory you are presently tapping on. It's actually a good sign. It means EFT is working!

You can approach this scenario in two different ways. Option one is to continue tapping on the present issue, hopefully getting it to a zero SUDS. Option two is to stop tapping on this specific issue and gently tap on any acupuncture point, asking the Holy Spirit prayerfully what is the event or memory underneath that has suddenly brought up even more emotion than you began with.

The Holy Spirit will tell you. Take that memory and go back to the beginning of these instructions and start again, dealing with this new issue. What is happening here is the Holy Spirit is doing the work for you by prioritizing what you need to tap about first. He's organizing your tapping procession. By following His cues, you will get your biggest tapping bang for your time. Remember, He knows you inside and out, what makes you tick, and what is holding you back from doing what God wants you to be doing. Just allow the Holy Spirit to lead you! Let Him be in charge!

Following is an example of my client friend Janice who isn't a practitioner, but who is willing to allow God to use her to help others with in-the-moment emotional needs.

Janice has taken my EFT class in Milwaukee for the sole purpose of learning how to tap for herself and her family—little did she know God had bigger plans for her! She stepped out in faith, in response to the Holy Spirit's call, and helped some of His "least" ones in a time of need (Matthew 18:6).

Here is Janice's story in her own words:

> I teach extracurricular activities. At the end of the year, we have a program so students can show their parents the new skills they have learned.
>
> A couple of weeks ago, one of my students, Molly, a wonderful, sweet, sensitive ten-year-old told me she just couldn't do the program. She couldn't learn the skills. Molly suffers from PANDA'S disease. PANDA'S

is an autoimmune response to a strep infection. It is diagnosed when a child develops behavioral or physical symptoms after an infection. Molly feels it interferes with her learning.

After learning EFT from Sherrie, I have used it only for my family and myself. However, the Holy Spirit gave me some confidence, so I decided to tap with Molly. We did the set up on the karate chop point: "Even if I think I cannot learn this material, I'm still an awesome kid." Suddenly, Molly's insights kicked in. She stopped and said, "This is a pressure point like acupuncture." I was amazed. How did she know that? I showed her the tapping points and she tapped where I showed her without saying anything. Her next comment was she could think better now and could master the skills needed for the program. Molly decided she could tap at school. I showed her the finger points, and she came up with the idea of tapping under her desk so she wouldn't disturb the teacher who she described as "harsh." Molly came up with her own statement: "Even if I feel I can't do it, I'm the greatest kid."

At the next practice, Molly's first comments were, "I can't do this." I began tapping without saying anything and Molly joined in with her words, "I'm the greatest kid." She was then able to practice and did a good job with the skills.

Molly told me she would miss a practice because she had to have two teeth extracted. She told me that the last time this was done, she threw up after they took the "green thing" off her nose. Oh boy! Another opportunity to tap. Molly laughed when we said, "I don't need to throw up."

Molly sailed through the dental procedure and her only complaint was she tried to eat applesauce while her gum was still bleeding and blood and applesauce didn't taste good together!

Two days before the program, Molly's mom called. Molly and her program partner had tried practicing at home for one part of the presentation with disastrous results. Mom said she would understand if I wanted to skip that part of the program. I gave her my "let's wait and see" speech because I really wanted Molly to participate.

That day at practice, I introduced Molly's program partner to EFT. While this was not a very long session, Molly felt better that her partner now also knew the "Power Tapping Game," as I call it.

Fast forward to the day of the program—Molly came in a bit apprehensive, but willing to give it a go. As we settled in, I began tapping and soon Molly followed suit. When it was her turn, Molly stepped forward confidently and did a beautiful job. The smile she flashed at the end was amazing. Mom thought it was a miracle!

I say that the Holy Spirit opened Sherrie's heart to teach her EFT, so she could teach me, so I could teach Molly a life-long skill.

Children really do clear quickly during tapping. It often happens in a fraction of the time it takes adults to benefit from EFT work because kids haven't built up layers and layers of rejection and rebuffing over the decades as many adults have.

I have produced four different YouTube videos about tapping with children. You can find the videos at https://www.youtube.com/channel/UCmxsHG9CFSWot 3rDZac2rSw/videos?sort=dd&view=0&shelf_id=1

Once you have mastered the initial tapping skills, begin to apply them to anything and everything in your life that feels distressful to you.

Remember, sometimes you might tap into deeply painful memories that may require tapping assistance from a qualified Christian EFT practitioner, and if needed I can supply you with names of trained Christian practitioners, both male and female.

Follow the instructions and watch our Lord change your feelings which can then change your life!

CHAPTER 9

Jenga®, Quantum Mechanics, and Your Emotional Life

Our emotional life is a great big Jenga® game! I make this connection to show you how the game can shed light on how our core emotional issues and all their competing aspects look like from this perspective. In case you aren't familiar with Jenga®, here is how the game plays:

> Jenga® is a game of physical and mental skill. Built on the simple premise of stacking blocks, Jenga® engages players of all ages, across all cultures. Jenga®'s success rests on its solid play value. Players take turns to remove a block (54 wooden blocks; each block is 3 times as longs as it is wide, and slightly smaller in height than in width) from a tower and balance it on top, creating a taller and increasingly unstable structure as the game progresses.
>
> Leslie Scott, game designer and author, developed the original Jenga® Classic game from a wood block stacking game her family had created in Ghana in the 1970s. Introduced to the public at the famous Harrods department store in London in 1982, Jenga® was launched in North America in 1986, and has since become an international game icon."[30]

Your emotional life is a collection of Jenga® block stack sets. Large layered pieces of plywood sit on top of stacked blocks creating Jenga® towers, holding up the plywood like an immense building complex. The plywood boards, layered one on top of another, are your core issues, which consist of beliefs that run your life from

---

30 http://jenga.com/about.php

a subconscious level. You have absolutely no idea the boards are there, what they actually mean, nor their significance to your life. The individual game blocks are all the negative aspects—the details from thoughts, sensory information, physical feelings, and distinct and unique emotions—that buttress your core problems. Depending on your emotional state, you may have only a few Jenga® sets, or you might have hundreds of them. Only your subconscious mind and God really know how many exist.

You begin this emotional game of Jenga® by tapping. As you pull out individual blocks, whether near the top of the structure or near the base, the overall structure becomes unstable, eventually crumbling into a heap. In your emotional journey, when you have dug out and nullified sufficient numbers of blocks (aspects), collapsing sufficient numbers of your own personal "Jenga®s," God can change your life. As your blocks are removed (neutralized) the entire structure of your life completely changes. You will open up different possibilities or ideas of how your life can look. Now, God has your attention. He often offers you other suggestions or notions of how you could live your life for Him.

GOD OF ALL POSSIBILITIES

While I'm no quantum physicist, I do enjoy reading about the subject, and I believe science offers another piece of the EFT puzzle that explains how God put this all together to work so well.

The Jenga® example explains how tapping works emotionally, but God's quantum mechanics (QM) explains why it seems to work.

Besides the wave function collapse principle that I'm about to explain, there was the QM principle of entanglement that also explains why we believe surrogate tapping works. That was discussed in chapter 7. Perhaps this entanglement idea is why forgiveness works so well, as when Jesus forgave his tormenters as He hung on the Cross in Luke 23:34," Jesus said, 'Father, forgive them, for they do not know what they are doing.' And they divided up his clothes by casting lots." QM seems to show that two separate entities are intertwined and influence each other even at great distances. We forgive; God applies the QM principle.

QM (also called quantum physics or quantum theory) is a branch of science that studies the physics of material objects at the atomic level versus the study of what I call classic physics in which Newton's Laws of Motion are predominant. In other words, the difference between these two branches are that QM operates on a *micro*, or smaller, perspective and classic physics sees the world from a *macro*, or larger, perspective.[31]

QM has broken down atoms into even smaller particles like quarks, leptons (muons, electron, neutrinos) and bosons; however, it has gone even further when earlier 20th-century studies showed that streams of particles called photons acted differently than single particles. These photons exhibit wave-like properties and are often called wavicles. Quantum physics theorizes a wavelike reality where things we think we see don't have definitive properties, even though we seem to experience a world of defined properties. Often, atoms are in two places at the same time. I look at it as a God-like ability. Jesus popped in and out of the Apostles' lives after the Resurrection, appearing out of nowhere, several times (Luke 24:36–46; John 20:19), even to the point where the Apostles thought Him to be a ghost.

Howard Van Till, a physics professor at Calvin College in Grand Rapids, Michigan, stated, "There is more to reality than the physical alone."[32] Most physicists don't deal in the spiritual concepts of creation; however, we need both perspectives of physical and spiritual to make sense of what happens around us.

What this means to the average person on the street is these photons don't behave as scientists once thought they did. They often are unpredictable. Out of this new information have emerged many other theories about how physics truly works. This science has opened up new areas of study. Frankly, as I read about it, I realize more and more how amazing our God truly is. Each and every time we think we are about to figure out Who and What God is, He throws another wrench into our scientific arena, pushing us to think harder and deeper than ever before in our history.

The specific QM law that I want to discuss here is wave function collapse. Hang in here with me because this isn't as difficult as it may sound.

The definition of wave function collapse in its simplest terms is: All possible solutions or probabilities are reduced to a single choice when observed. Werner Heisenberg introduced the concept in 1927 when he wrote a paper on the uncertainty principle. Now, please note there are variations of the variations of many of these laws and principles as scientists perform and repeat their experiments. I, however, want to apply a spiritual principle to this quantum mechanics law.

---

31   Leaf, *How to Switch on Your Brain*, 104–106.
32   Jeeves, Science, *Life and Christian Belief*, 67.

Again, it is my interpretation, but to me it makes sense scripturally. Nothing is impossible with God (Luke 1:37; Mark 10:27; Matthew 19:26). We can do all things through Christ Who strengthens us (Philippians 4:13). In the story of the mustard seed, Jesus reminds us we only need a teeny tiny scrap of belief and we can move a mountain (Matthew 17:20). God continually reminds us that He is the God of the impossible (Jeremiah 32:27; Mark 11:24; Luke 18:27; Romans 8:31; Job 42:2; Genesis 18:14). Do you also remember the story of Abraham, Sarah, and God's promise of a son to them? God also states He will do as He pleases (Isaiah 46:10). He is God after all!

We are given free will. We choose to follow God or we choose to disobey Him. He never forces His will on us; we are given a choice in how we run our life.

If the wave function collapse law is true, and I believe that it is, we have multitudes of choices each day in all avenues of our lives. This is free will.[33]

Let me give you an example. When you awaken in the morning, your day is open to you. You may have to go to work, but whether you choose to go or not is a choice. Do you plan to arrive at the appointed work time? Will you wear your red dress or blue suit? Will you part your hair to the right or to the left? Do you take a lunch or do you eat in the cafeteria? Will you obey the speed limit? Should you stop at McDonald's for that mocha you like so much? Do you drive the freeway or will you take 35th Street today? Do I pray now or do I pray while driving?

Do you see my point? Every habit may have hundreds or thousands of variations to it. You can choose to think God's thoughts, holy and wholesome, or you can choose to dismiss Him, His Words, and His promises for your life, allowing satan to deceive you into thinking you are in control of your life, running it better than your Lord can. Once you make a choice, you have just collapsed the wave function into that single possibility. There's no going back. There are no do-overs. The choice has been made. Now you live with that choice. You can never return to that exact moment in the past when a decision was made and change your mind. The present has slipped into the past, headed for eternity.

We human beings like homeostasis—the state of equilibrium or relative calm. We hate change! We are habitual creatures, doing the same thing again and again, day after day. We have convinced ourselves we like it that way. Frankly, it is our subconscious mind that keeps us in that homeostatic state, or it tries to.

---

33 Leaf, *How to Switch on Your Brain*, 106–107.

The subconscious mind hates change. Robert Collier (1885–1950) once said:

> Our subconscious minds have no sense of humor, play no jokes, and cannot tell the difference between reality and an imagined thought or image.[34]

Because the subconscious mind knows no difference between imagination and reality, it keeps us stuck in patterns that aren't in our best interest. Our perceptions of situations around us create our habits and our behaviors. Often this conduct is sinful.[35]

When we are busy to distraction, we are taking the law of wave function collapse to its end. As we consider solutions to our life's problems, we are pre-occupied with issues immediately before us that we rarely have the time to consider the outcome that follows the choices we make. We don't have time to consider the implications of what we are about to do. Having a vision in life is important to making godly decisions. If we cannot see where we are moving towards, does it then matter whether our actions are moral or immoral?

Many times we think we have no other choices. All the possibilities God offers to solve problems in our life collapse into a single choice that we tend to repeat again and again because it feels comfortable, and the subconscious mind literally sabotages us into re-enacting the same behavior.

This isn't a conscious thought on your part, but it is held together by your early implanted neurobiology. Those neurochemicals that were produced in negative childhood memories are still running your life today. The proof and evidence are in your unchanging behavior, sometimes, even sinful or immoral life choices.

Your subconscious decision to repeat your behavior has trapped you. Please know I'm not blaming you. Again, this is *not* your fault. You are a "victim" of your own chemistry and the teachings you were given decades ago (Proverbs 22:6). But it **IS** your responsibility to change your attitudes and your behavior to something much more Christ-like as part of the process of sanctification.

---

34 https://www.brainyquote.com/quotes/authors/r/robert_collier.html
35 Virkler Kayembe and Rice Smith, *EFT for Christians*, 48.

Positive change is now up to you, and you're well on your way because you picked up this book! God might be telling you to consider EFT to change some of those annoyingly sinful habits that are interfering with your relationship with Him.

Right here, right now, another wave function collapse has just occurred. You probably have tried a multitude of different spiritual and emotional remedies—most of them to no avail, or you wouldn't still be looking for a solution to fix how badly you feel inside your soul. Many proposed remedies are available, but now you've chosen the idea of EFT as a possible corrective measure.

When we tap, God opens up all kinds of possibilities. He has good moral solutions to every one of our human dilemmas. He is omniscient. But we have continued to make the same choices, hoping the outcome would be different. Albert Einstein's definition of insanity is apropos here: "Insanity is doing the same thing over and over again and expecting different results." Dr. Einstein was describing the human condition!

As an example, I often hear women who tap with me say they married an alcoholic, swearing they will never make that mistake again. Low and behold, they often find out later in their next marriage they again married an alcoholic or drug addict. These women usually ask, "What is going on here?" They hesitate to look again for a stable marriage partner for fear they will once again be duped.

What is happening to these women—or to anyone who has faults (sins) or who is perceived to have a character defect—is their neurochemistry has trapped them into the behavior. It has little to do with being weak willed, as many pre-Sigmund Freud psychiatrists believed in the 19th century. It's all in the chemistry of how God created us.

Originally, prior to the Fall in the Garden of Eden, this chemistry was meant for good. It kept humanity stable and in a joyful and peaceful place where there was no need to change or to look for other solutions. Adam and Eve walked in the cool of the evening with God in the Garden. How much better could it get?

After the Fall, our God-created chemistry continued to protect man from the evil in the world by alerting him when danger was abreast. The adrenaline and cortisol rose to meet the dangerous physical situation so man could fight or run away—Flight or Fight Response—as the situation deemed.

Today, at least in western culture, we no longer face a dangerous environment, so our worst enemy now is worry, fear, and concern for those around us and for our future. That highly charged neurochemistry, the same grouping of neurobiological chemicals as Adam and Eve's, eats away at our internal organs and wears down our immune system.

As Robert Collier stated earlier, our subconscious mind doesn't distinguish between the real physical danger of a mugger and worrying about the possibility of a mugger attacking us. And the body runs the same high-intensity chemicals throughout our system in the same extreme amounts in both scenarios. Physical danger and worry are equal in the eye of our subconscious mind. Physical danger can kill us for obvious reasons, and worry can kill us by destroying our immune system.

By using EFT, you go back into the negative issues of your childhood and your young adult life—and also any huge mishaps in adulthood—disarming your neurochemistry through actual tapping informing your subconscious mind you are now safe today, knowing in your mind the bad situations indeed happened in the past.

Dr. Van der Kolk addresses this idea with these thoughts:

> However, traumatized people chronically feel unsafe inside their bodies: The past is alive in the form of gnawing interior discomfort. Their bodies are constantly bombarded by visceral warning signs, and, in an attempt to control these processes, they often become an expert at ignoring their gut feelings and in numbing awareness of what is played out inside. They learn to hide from their selves.[36]

Remember, your mind is your body, and by releasing these negative experiences from every cell of your body, you are improving your immunity and giving your body a chance to heal.

Carolyn Myss is not a Christian, but she understands the relationship between how God created our mind and body to work together, giving us life in the truest and best sense there is. Myss said:

---

36 Van der Kolk, *The Body Keeps the Score*, 96-97.

"Our experiences, positive and negative, register a memory in cell tissue as well as in the energy field. Neuropeptides, the chemicals triggered by emotions, are thoughts converted into matter... your mind is in every cell of your body."[37]

Those neuropeptides, along with hormones and neurotransmitters, solidify difficult memories into our very cells, damaging them. Tapping appears to reverse that process, clearing them, allowing the cells to heal.

Our God is a God of possibilities. He has endless solutions to our human plight. He suggests many of them in Scripture and within the Ten Commandments. He gave us these instructions for our good. Sadly, we humans make mistakes. For our spiritual mistakes, God the Father sent Jesus to the Cross to atone for our sins. But for all the ramifications on the physical end of this spectrum, He gave us energy techniques, one of which is Emotional Freedom Techniques.

Let me illustrate with a story.

Sandra is well into her 8th decade of life, having been diagnosed with a neurological health issue 40 years ago. She functions well, but often worries incessantly about her sons and her grandchildren, and she has a difficult relationship with her ex-daughter-in-law.

Even though she had no idea what tapping was, she trusted me enough to agree to try it, probably out of curiosity more than anything else.

We tapped via telephone about every situation that was driving her to distraction about her ex-daughter-in-law, Maggie. Probably 45 minutes into her tirade, she suddenly stopped talking. I inquired as to what was going on. Sandra exclaimed, "Oh, my goodness. I never thought to try this with Maggie!" I asked what "this" was, and she continued telling me the Holy Spirit had just given her a wonderful idea of exactly what to say to Maggie the next time she called complaining about her job and her ex-husband, Sandra's son.

During tapping, God had revealed to Sandra another possible solution to her relationship with Maggie. The thought came to Sandra in the moment while tapping when she was in a lower brain wave state in which the subconscious mind opens a small portal to our conscious mind. Sandra was totally amazed.

---

37 Myss, *Anatomy of the Spirit*, 35.

Months later, I inquired how her relationship with Maggie was progressing since our tapping session. Sandra was so pleased because Maggie had ceased phoning frequently to whine about one thing or another. This gave Sandra some much-needed space in her life and peace too.

Now, Sandra still continues to live in her own home, tapping and praying as I taught her to do. She's slowing down a bit, she tells me, but is still doing her daily routines in an adequate manner.

Following is another story of what God can do when we break down our static neurobiological channels.

Joan, nearly 70, called me to tap about some issues in her life. As with many people in their senior years, relationships often are the bugaboo—children, grandchildren, and, sometimes, great-grandchildren all complicate kinships.

As we tapped on some health issues, upcoming medical procedures, and all the fears and anxiousness around them, Joan managed to pull out some childhood similarities to what she was feeling in the tapping moment. The Holy Spirit, as always, was faithful to help us make those mindful connections and then neutralize them to open up new potentialities of change as we go forward in our lives.

The Holy Spirit didn't let Joan down. Weeks later, after the zaniness of medical tests and procedures and returning life to some normalcy, Joan let me in on a new secret. She had begun to write poetry again. In subduing the emotional turmoil she held in her mind-body, a new creative path opened to her. She has now even begun to pursue a publisher for some of her new work and some older compositions, too. Isn't our Lord amazing?

I've seen this same tapping outgrowth occur again and again in different women in different stages—and ages—in life. God does have a specific project for you in this life. What is He purposing you to do for His Kingdom? Tapping out the old patterns may open up that doorway, revealing His plan for your life.

Don't limit God. He is your very best friend, encourager, and cheerleader! He wants you to succeed. He wants your life to be filled with peace and joy. You are His tool to communicate these traits and virtues to others around you, allowing them to visualize how Jesus has impacted your life both today on earth and your future in heaven.

Use tapping to open up and expand new ideas around your old thought patterns of rejection and contradictions. Our God is the God of possibilities and solutions. When wave function collapse occurs in our lives, and it will, we continue to use the same worn-out solutions and quick fixes, we hinder God, reducing Him to that same worn-out answer that probably isn't working well for either us or Him.

Reopen future prospects by tapping on the old habits that have painted you into that same corner of your life. Let God liven up your creative juices to reinvigorate you with new ideas and potentialities.

Our God is unchanging (Hebrews 13:8) and that trait of His cements Romans 8:28–31 in place forever. I know He is faithful to do this. I'm living proof. And you can be, too. Begin your EFT journey today, asking God to show you how to apply it in your life, and asking Him to open up in your life all the possibilities He has waiting for you.

God gives us a second chance to change our lives and, inadvertently, to change also the lives of everyone around us. Start tapping and dismantling those Jenga® blocks from your emotional life. By unlocking those old neural patterns of childhood through tapping, often God opens up something completely different in your life. He loves to surprise you with the unexpected! I hope you are willing to allow Him to do this for you. Let God be God.

CHAPTER 10

Scriptures for Tapping: Wisdom and Psalms

Each of us has Bible verse favorites. Most of us want to hear God say something positive and uplifting to us. We tend to ignore the heavy admonition type verses because they feel painful to hear. In this chapter, I am including two different Scripture verse themes or paraphrases. These verses are pulled mostly from the New International Version. Remember, use these verses after you have tapped out the negative emotions associated with the memory or event you have worked on.

Tapping negatively is heavy-duty work. We have heard for decades to repeat positive affirmations about ourselves and situations around us. Dr. Gabor Maté explains why positive affirmations simply don't work:

> As Dr. Michael Kerr points out, "compulsive optimism is one of the ways we bind our anxiety to avoid confronting it. That form of positive thinking is the coping mechanism of the hurt child. The adult who remains hurt without being aware of it makes this residual defence of the hurt into a life principle." He continues, "Even more fundamentally, *not posing those questions is itself a source of stress* (author's emphasis). First, 'positive thinking' is based on an unconscious belief that we are not strong enough to handle reality. Allowing this fear to dominate engenders a state of childhood apprehension. Whether or not the apprehension is conscious, it is a state of stress."[38]

---

38 Maté, *When the Body Says NO*, 244–245.

If the advice of positive thinking had worked well, we wouldn't now be discussing EFT at all! Dr. Maté goes on further to explain how this stress of denying our problems through positive thinking triggers our HPA axis response, allowing our life to be run by these subconscious fears and thoughts—often destroying our health.

I've discussed the HPA axis stress response briefly in *EFT for Christians, Tapping in God's Peace and Joy*.[39] The problem with positive thinking is that a positive thought really isn't what we believe or are truly thinking; therefore, we are deceiving ourselves. As Scripture reminds us in 1 John 1:8–10:

> If we claim to be without sin, we deceive ourselves and the truth is not in us. If we confess our sins, He is faithful and just and will forgive us our sins and purify us from all unrighteousness. If we claim we have not sinned, we make Him out to be a liar and his word is not in us.

To some extent, this is exactly what we Christians do when we use EFT. Instead of deceiving ourselves into thinking we are wonderful, great, loving, kind, and charitable people by repeating positive affirmations, we get down in the dirt, tapping out our hearts to God, confessing our misdeeds and faults, repenting and asking for His forgiveness. To do otherwise is indeed making God out to be a liar. This is one of the ways satan deceives us (1 Peter 5:8) by keeping us locked up in our emotional pain, telling us God doesn't love us and that there is no way out of this mess we find ourselves in.

God is faithful and not only to forgive our sins, but also to heal us physically and emotionally. He wants to heal us. We are His children. He wants the very best for us always.

So, do **NOT** use these Bible verses as an alternative to negative tapping work. Once all the negative feelings have been tapped out of emotional or physical issues, feel free to tap these POSITIVE scriptural truths, allowing God to refresh your body, mind, and soul.

Matthew 12:43–45 is often used to explain that we need to keep our spiritual house in order. Once we have given our life to Jesus in an act of regeneration, we must keep that relationship in good order. To keep a relationship healthy, we must have fellowship and communication with God as we do in human relationships.

---

39 Virkler Kayembe and Rice Smith, *EFT for Christians*, 53–54.

I created these tapping lists, first, to help fill that now emptied out space in a Christian's emotional psyche. Let God replace all the negative emotions and thoughts. We have no reason to give satan a foothold to enter again with more destructive thoughts and ideas, bringing more pain and hurt to us. Fill yourself with Jesus. He is our sufficiency (Colossians 2:10).

Second, I have found, on occasion, that a client will simply tell me after an especially intense tapping session they feel "empty and exhausted." Nothing is more refreshing than to fill up those tired and alone places in our heart than with the Word of God. Therefore, use these verses to refresh yourself after a long, and possibly, dramatic tapping session, letting God hold your heart and pour His power and might into your life.

TAPPING WISDOM

I've pulled the following verses primarily from the Old Testament, where some of the most profound verses are written about Who our God is and about how much He loves us.

The Lord's Name is my strong tower (Proverbs 18:10).
O, God, you are my God; I will praise you forever (Isaiah 25:1).
The plans of the diligent lead to profit (Proverbs 21:5).
I am part of God's mighty Kingdom (Hosea 2:22).
God honors me as I stand in His presence (Lamentations 2:2b).
I know that God can do all things (Job 42:1).
I have God's strength like that of a lion (Hosea 5:13b).
I rejoice, day after day, always filled with His presence (Proverbs 8:30).
I trust in My Lord; He is ever present with me (Isaiah 25:9b).
My innermost being rejoices when Your lips speak what is right and good (Proverbs 23:16).
God performs wonders that cannot be fathomed (Job 5:9).
I am the Lord your God who stands ever before you to defend you (Isaiah 41:10).
Always I keep His Words in my heart and on my mind (Proverbs 5:21b).
I live constantly in God's holy presence (Hosea 6:2).
Love justice, think of the Lord in goodness, and seek Him in integrity of heart (Wisdom 1:1).
I will remember that the Lord's purpose is what prevails (Proverbs 19:21).
God keeps my heart and mind in perfect peace (Isaiah 26:3).
I follow the Lord all the days of my life (Hosea 11:10).
I am restored by God (Job 33:26b).

Better is a neighbor at hand than a brother far away (Proverbs 27:10b).

I am strong in the Lord (Lamentations 1:13).

The Lord of the Universe is my God (Hosea 12:9).

The Spirit of the Lord fills the world, is all-embracing, and knows what man says (Wisdom 1:7).

Above all else, I guard my heart, for it is the wellspring of my life (Proverbs 5:23).

I am the crown of splendor in the Lord's hand because I am made in His image and likeness (Isaiah 62:2).

I will be secure because there is hope in God, my Savior (Job 11:18).

God's Word is a shield to me, giving me refuge whenever I am in need (Proverbs 30:5).

He who professes to have knowledge of the Lord is a child of God (Wisdom 2:13).

As iron sharpens iron, so a Christian friend sharpens you (Proverbs 27:17).

I tell of the kindnesses of the Lord and He lifts me up and carries me with the same kindness (Isaiah 63:7–9).

My heart and mind are strong in the Lord (Lamentations 1:20).

I am whole because Your hands shaped me and made me (Job 10:8).

God's Word is life to me and health to my body (Proverbs 5:22).

I seek the Lord while He may be found, and I ponder all His holy Words (Isaiah 55:6).

God gives me wisdom, knowledge, and happiness (Ecclesiastes 2:26).

I am guided by God's integrity (Proverbs 11:3).

God formed man to be imperishable; the image of His own nature He made me (Wisdom 2:23).

My Lord gives me abundant joy and peace (Isaiah 58:14).

I wait upon the Lord and He will direct all my paths (Hosea 12:6b).

My Savior upholds me with His righteousness (Lamentations 2:3).

He who confesses and forsakes his sins prospers (Proverbs 28:13).

I will rejoice in the Lord and be glad for He is my Savior (Joel 1:23).

My life is in God's care (Lamentations 2:12).

Your providence watches over my spirit (Job 10:12b).

God always works wonders for me in my life (Joel 2:26).

The Lord prospers all that I do when I hold tight to His hand, walking in all His ways (Isaiah 53:19b).

Blessed is he who trusts in the Word of the Lord (Proverbs 16:20b).

I, the Lord, uphold you with My righteous right hand (Isaiah 41:10b).

By God's grace I am made whole again (Lamentations 2:4).

I see God's righteousness and compassion for me (Micah 7:9, 14).

My victory rests with my Lord (Proverbs 21:31b).

The just live forever, and in the Lord is their recompense, and the thought of them is with the Most High (Wisdom 5:15).

I wait for the Lord and He will deliver me (Proverbs 20:22).

The Holy Spirit infuses my soul with virtues (Joel 2:28).

God is my healer (Lamentations 2:13).

The Lord goes before me; The God of Israel is my rear guard, protecting me in all things (Isaiah 52:12b).

I am a friend of God (Lamentations 2:5).

He will fill my mouth with laughter and my lips with shouts of joy (Job 8:21).

God is my shield from all my enemies (Lamentations 2:16).

I trust in the Lord with all my heart and lean not on my own understanding (Proverbs 3:5).

God of my fathers has made all things by Your Word (Wisdom 9:1).

I sing out joyfully from my heart because of all that He has done for me (Isaiah 65:14).

A joyful heart is health to the body (Proverbs 17:22).

I walk humbly with my God (Micah 6:8b).

God is my rampart and my fortress in Whom I trust (Lamentations 2:8).

I recognize that whatever God does endures forever (Ecclesiastes 3:11).

You have mercy on me because You can do all things (Wisdom 11:23).

I will obey You so that I can dwell in security, peace, and without fear of harm (Proverbs 1:33).

God binds up all my wounds (Job 5:18).

I am a precious jewel in God's sight (Isaiah 43:3b).

God is my sure foundation at all times (Isaiah 33:6).

I am set free by the blood and resurrection of Christ (Lamentations 2:9).

He who has compassion for the poor lends to the Lord, and He will repay him for his good deeds (Proverbs 19:17).

God shelters me from the wind and He is my refuge from the storm (Isaiah 32:2).

I listen to my Father's instructions so that I may gain His understanding (Proverbs 4:1).

Our God is true and good, slow to anger, and governing all with mercy (Wisdom 15:1).

A true friend is more loyal than a brother (Proverbs 18:24).

God is my only peace and security (Micah 5:4–5).

I am forgiven by the Blood of the Lamb (Lamentations 2:10).

God gives breath to His people and life to those who walk in faith (Isaiah 42:5b).

I know that everything God does will endure forever (Ecclesiastes 3:13).
My God is my refuge and strength all day long (Joel 3:16).
Wisdom and knowledge from the Lord pleases my heart (Proverbs 2:10).
God leads me to all truth and righteousness (Lamentations 2:14).
I dwell in righteousness and peace that comes only from the Lord on high (Isaiah 32:16)
The crucible for silver and the furnace for gold, but the tester of hearts is the Lord (Proverbs 17:3).
God pledges His faithfulness, truth, and mercy to me daily (Micah 7:20).
I stand in awe of God (Ecclesiastes 5:7b).
God answers me before I even ask as He knows all my needs (Isaiah 65:24).
I honor God with my first fruits of all my income (Proverbs 3:9).
God is my only source of strength; my help comes only from Him, in Whom I trust (Isaiah 28:8b).
Many are the plans in a man's heart, but it is the decision of the Lord that endures (Proverbs 19:21).
I only trust in the name of the Lord and rely on my God (Isaiah 50:10b).
God's wonders abound around me; I watch for the miracles (Joel 2:30).
I am determined to be wise (Ecclesiastes 7:23).
I keep my eyes straight ahead and my glance directed forward, so my feet never slip (Proverbs 4:25–26).
God provides me quietness and confidence in my faith as I rest in Him (Isaiah 32:16b)
Trust in the Lord and He will help you (Proverbs 20:22).
My God stands with me and shepherds me (Micah 5:4).
Gladness and joy will overtake me as I ponder the wonders of the God of the Universe (Isaiah 51:11b).
God's beauty and joy reside in me (Lamentations 2:15).
Remember, I am the Lord your God (Joel 3:12).
You, Oh, Lord, are the Potter and we are the clay; mold us to Your image (Wisdom 15:7).
God keeps my foot from stumbling and my path straight (Proverbs 3:23).
The Lord speaks to Me and guides me in my every step (Isaiah 28:11).
The King takes delight in honest lips, and the man who speaks what is right He loves (Proverbs 16:13).
I turned my mind to understand, to investigate, to search out wisdom (Ecclesiastes 7:25).
I will remember my Lord's teachings and keep in mind at all times His commands (Proverbs 3:1).

God strengthens my feeble hands and steadies my knees whenever my strength fails me (Isaiah 35:3).

A lamp from the Lord is the breath of man; it searches through his inmost being (Proverbs 20:27).

God gave me faithfulness, love, and acknowledgment because He created me (Hosea 4:1b).

God's purpose always stands, and I bear witness to His righteousness at all times (Isaiah 46:10b).

My path is like the shining Light that grows in brilliance till the perfect day (Proverbs 4:18).

You, my God, are my Savior; You have put all my sins behind Your back to be seen no more (Isaiah 38:17).

To practice justice is a joy for the just (Proverbs 21:15).

God's Holy Spirit fills me up to capacity (Micah 3:8).

The Lord comforts me at all times; In His arms I rest securely (Isaiah 49:13b).

I see all that God has done and it is good (Ecclesiastes 8:17).

God gathers me in His everlasting arms and comforts me (Micah 2:12).

I bind fidelity and kindness around my neck (Proverbs 3:3).

My soul yearns for you, Oh, God, as a child pines for its mother (Isaiah 26:8b).

The eyes of the Lord are in every place, keeping watch (Proverbs 15:3).

I am the Lord your God, and I teach you what is best for you. Listen to me (Isaiah 48:17b).

He who pursues justice and kindness will find life and honor (Proverbs 21:21).

I walk with a joyful heart (Ecclesiastes 9:7).

I am attentive to God's Holy Word for they are health to my whole being (Proverbs 4:20–22).

God is my Rock and Salvation; in Him I will stand firm all the days to my life (Isaiah 44:8b).

The Lord loves the pure of heart (Proverbs 22:11).

I will return to Him for He has redeemed Me from all unrighteousness (Isaiah 44:22).

God promises happiness to me if I obey Him (Proverbs 8:33).

Wisdom is better than strength (Ecclesiastes 9:16).

A good name is more desirable than great riches, and high esteem than gold and silver (Proverbs 22:1).

I am filled with God's glory and power by His Holy Spirit (Micah 3:8).

God instructs me in new things previously unknown to me as I open my heart and mind to Him (Isaiah 48:6b).

I walk honestly and securely because the Lord is my Shepherd (Proverbs 10:9).

I know that God is the Maker of all things (Ecclesiastes 11:3).

I wait for You while You level my path, making straight all my ways (Isaiah 26:7–8).

The Lord will defend our cause (Proverbs 22:23).

The good man wins favor from God (Proverbs 12:2).

My glad heart lights up my face (Proverbs 15:13).

I am happy and God gives my heart joy (Ecclesiastes 11:9).

Our Redeemer is strong and He will defend you (Proverbs 23:11).

The Lord is a stronghold to him who walks honestly (Proverbs 10:29).

I will follow the ways of God's heart (Ecclesiastes 11:9b).

Pleasing words are a honeycomb, sweet to the taste and healthful to the body (Proverbs 16:24).

By Wisdom is a house built, by understanding it is made firm (Proverbs 24:3).

Truthful lips endure forever (Proverbs 12:19).

As the heavens in height and the earth in depth, the heart of our King is unfathomable (Proverbs 25:3).

My mind is steadfast, dwelling in perfect peace (Isaiah 26:3b).

A cheerful glance brings joy to the heart; good news invigorates the bones (Proverbs 15:30).

The Lord is the Maker of us all, rich and poor (Proverbs 22:2).

You have chosen me as Your special jewel. I am Yours forever, resting in Your mighty arms (Isaiah 41:9b).

TAPPING PSALMS

Because King David expressed so much emotion during his life and in his psalms, I've chosen a selection of Psalms that I find comforting to my soul when I feel distressed, dismayed, disappointed, or even depressed.

Again, when after tapping a void inside us appears, I believe the emptiness comes from the removal of the emotions we have borne for years. Suddenly, they are gone. A hole appears in their place. Occasionally, I want something to fill that void; other times, it feels good to simply be emptied out. Situations fluctuate and emotions change with each EFT tapping experience.

If you find any of these statements difficult to say or they don't feel true to you, then you may have just found more tapping fodder. These statements should ring true for us as Christians. If they don't, I would explore why that is, tapping out whatever negative emotions lie around the statement(s). Physiology teaches us that it takes about three weeks to secure new neural connections, so I suggest tapping these Scripture verses for at least that amount of time. If that emotional hole seems to linger, tap them longer if you so desire. Reinforcing them into your spiritual subconscious can't do anything but help to embed them permanently.

If you have finished the difficult work of tapping, then have some tapping fun and dwell on how God impacts your life as you say each positive statement.

I delight in the law of the Lord and I will keep His commandments (Psalm 1:1).

I trust in the Lord and do good so I may inherit the land (Psalm 37:3).

I yield much Christian fruit for Christ (Psalm 1:3).

I will proclaim the decrees of the Lord (Psalm 2:7).

God provides all my earthly needs (Psalm 81:16).

I will serve the Lord with fear and rejoicing (Psalm 2:11).

God counsels and instructs me in the way I should go (Psalm 32:8).

I wait patiently for the Lord; He will answer me (Psalm 37:34).

My Lord is enthroned as King forever, and I will praise Him for all He has done for me (Psalm 29:10).

I lift up my head and know you are my shield and fortress (Psalm 3:3).

God is always with me no matter where I am (Psalm 73:23).

Happy am I who trusts in the Lord (Psalm 40:5).

I lie down and sleep in peace because the Lord sustains me (Psalm 3:5).

God guards my very life and I trust in Him (Psalm 86:2).

The Lord blesses me always (Psalm 3:8).

You are my Helper and Deliverer (Psalm 40:18).

I sought the Lord and He answered me and delivered me from all my fears (Psalm 34:5).

My Lord my God always hears my cry (Psalm 4:3).

My God is my Rock and my Salvation; in Him will I stand (Psalm 89:26).

The Lord's Light shines always upon my face (Psalm 4:6).

God's favor rests upon me because I am His redeemed (Psalm 90:17).

I sleep in peace because you make me dwell in safety (Psalm 4:8).

I bless the Name of the Lord God of Israel for all eternity. Amen (Psalm 41:14).

You, Lord, make straight all my paths (Psalm 5:8).

Do me justice, Oh God, and fight my fight against a faithless people who oppose You (Psalm 43:1).

My humble and contrite heart stands before you, Oh, God (Psalm 51:19).

My God protects me in all things as I do His will (Psalm 5:11).

Your throne stands forever and forever, and I shall worship before You (Psalm 45:7).

You are my King and My God who bestowed victories on Jacob (Psalm 44:5).

I trust in You, Oh, Lord, with my whole heart and soul (Psalm 55:24).

My God reigns over all the nations as He sits on His holy throne (Psalm 47:9).

I behold the deeds of the Lord for the astounding things He has wrought upon me (Psalm 46:9).

You have freed me from my blood guilt, Oh, Lord, through Jesus my Savior (Psalm 51:16).

My God will guide me forever and forever (Psalm 48:15).

I take courage and remain stouthearted while I hope in the Lord (Psalm 31:25).

God is my Helper; He sustains my soul (Psalm 54:6).

I am blessed by my Father in heaven (Psalm 5:12).

God's ministering angels protect me by day and by night (Psalm 91:11–12).

Every cry I utter is heard by my Savior (Psalm 6:9).

I chant Your praise among the peoples and the nations as I give You thanks for all You have done for me (Psalm 57:10).

I am glad in the Lord and give thanks to His Holy Name (Psalm 97:12).

I am accepted with all my faults by God (Psalm 6:10).

You have set me upon a high rock and You have given me rest (Psalm 61:3b).

My sins are cast by God as far as the east is from the west (Psalm 103:11).

I stand righteous because of Christ Jesus (Psalm 7:17).

God has provided an inheritance for me in heaven (Psalm 105:5).

I am crowned with glory and honor because of Christ (Psalm 8:5).

Your Word is the Light unto my path (Psalm 119:105).

The Lord knows my name and I put all my trust in Him (Psalm 9:10).

Oh, Lord, You are my God for Whom I pine and seek like parched land seeks water (Psalm 63:2).

God always remembers His covenant to me through Jesus His Son (Psalm 110:4–5).

I rejoice in Your Salvation (Psalm 9:14).

God keeps me from all harm; He always protects me (Psalm 121:7).

The Lord is my encouragement; He hears my every prayer
(Psalm 10:12).

I am filled with perfect joy because of what God has done for me
(Psalm 126:3).

The Lord protects my every move, seeking justice for me (Psalm 11:7).

The voice of the Lord is mighty and majestic, and I listen intently for all
His instructions (Psalm 29:4).

I wait for the Lord; my soul hopes in His Word (Psalm 130:5).

My gratitude overflows to the Lord for His goodness and overflowing
love toward me (Psalm 13:6).

I have a still and quiet soul as I rest in God, my Savior (Psalm 131:1–2).

God is present with me every minute of my life (Psalm 14:5).

I lift up my hands in the sanctuary and praise my God (Psalm 134:2).

God stands on my right side, keeping me steady (Psalm 16:8).

God's love for me endures forever (Psalm 136).

I am the apple of God's merciful eye (Psalm 17:8).

God preserves my life at all times (Psalm 138:7).

God is my Light and my Salvation (Psalm 18:28).

I lift up my voice to God; He hears when I cry out to Him about anything (Psalm 142:1).

God ransoms my life from all evils (Psalm 69:19).

I am armed with God's mighty strength (Psalm 18:32).

I open my lips all day long and proclaim your praise and glory, Oh,
God (Psalm 51:17).

God's right hand sustains me (Psalm 18:35).

Blessed be the Name of the Lord, both now and forevermore
(Psalm 113:2).

Our God is in Heaven; whatever He wills, He does for us
(Psalm 115:3).

I will give thanks to You, for You have answered me and have been my
Savior (Psalm 118:21).

God heals my broken heart and binds up all of my wounds
(Psalm 147:3).

I have God's help and support always (Psalm 20:2).

God's perfect peace abides in my heart as I live my life for Him
(Psalm 148–150).

My victory stands with Christ Jesus (Psalm 21:7).

Oh, God, you taught me from my youth until the present, and I proclaim Your wondrous deeds to me (Psalm 71:17).

I praise the Lord with all my soul and spirit (Psalm 22:25).

My God is my safety and my glory; He is the Rock of my strength, and in Him do I trust (Psalm 62:8).

You remember me when time comes for my heavenly inheritance through Jesus (Psalm 74:2).

God supplies all my needs (Psalm 23:1).

I chant praise to my Lord, extolling Him Who rides upon the clouds where I will join Him in glory (Psalm 68:5).

Keep me in your presence all day long, Oh, Lord, and instill more of Your Holy Spirit within me (Psalm 51:13).

I lie down in God's peace (Psalm 23:2).

Great are the works of the Lord, exquisite in all their delights (Psalm 111:2).

I give you thanks, Oh, Lord, and I invoke Your Name and declare Your wondrous deeds (Psalm 75:2).

My soul is constantly restored as I am guided by God along my path walk (Psalm 23:3).

My comfort lies in knowing God walks with me (Psalm 23:4).

I praise the name of Jesus with all my soul because His Name is good (Psalm 52:9).

God is my guardian and my shade in Whom I rest assured (Psalm 121:5).

I long for Your salvation, Oh, Lord, and Your law is my delight (Psalm 119:174).

God spreads a table before me with everything that I need (Psalm 23:5).

Oh, Lord, Your way is holy and blameless, and I will follow it forever (Psalm 77:14).

My cup overflows with goodness and mercy (Psalm 23:6).

Great is Your love toward me, Oh, Father, You Who created me (Psalm 57:10).

I dwell in the house of the Lord now and forever (Psalm 23:7).

I sing joyfully to God my strength; I acclaim the God of Jacob as my own (Psalm 81:2).

God guides me in all truth and I hope in Him (Psalm 25:5).

You are just, Lord, and your ordinances are right (Psalm 119:137).

I walk before my God in the Light of life (Psalm 56:13).

Create in me a clean heart, Oh, God, and renew a right spirit within me (Psalm 51:12).

God releases my feet from all snares (Psalm 25:15).

I know that You alone are the Most High over all of the earth, and You are my Savior (Psalm 83:19).

My life is filled with integrity and uprightness in God's hope (Psalm 25:21).

Give thanks to the Lord, for He is good; His mercy endures forever toward me (Psalm 118:29).

My feet constantly stand on level, solid ground (Psalm 26:12).

You are great and You do wondrous deeds; there is no one like You, Oh, God (Psalm 86:10).

Jesus is my Light; I have nothing to fear (Psalm 27:1).

I look to You to give me what I need at the proper time (Psalm 145:15).

I watch for You continuously, Oh, Lord, for You are my refuge and the love of my life (Psalm 59:9).

God exalts my head above my enemies (Psalm 27:6).

I am confident in God my Savior (Psalm 27:13).

My God is exalted above the heavens and over all the earth (Psalm 108:6).

I feel secure in my God (Psalm 30:6).

Oh, Lord, You are merciful toward me, and gracious, abounding in kindness and fidelity (Psalm 86:15).

I offer thanksgiving to my God with shouts of joy, declaring His works (Psalm 107:22).

My sins are completely covered by Jesus' Blood (Psalm 32:1).

He carries all my burdens faithfully (Psalm 68:19).

You are my stronghold and my deliverer (Psalm 144: 2).

I rest in the plans firmly set by my God (Psalm 33:11).

Oh, God, You are my refuge through all generations (Psalm 90:1).

I delight in the Lord and I wait for the desires of my heart when I ask (Psalm 37:4).

My heart is steadfast in You, Oh, God; my heart is steadfast (Psalm 108:2).

I stand in a firm place set before me by God (Psalm 40:2).

God defends me on my right hand and on my left hand from all my enemies (Psalm 74:22).

I am redeemed because of God's love (Psalm 44:26).

I rest still and quiet before the awesomeness of God (Psalm 46:19).

You make me glad, Oh, Lord, by the works of Your Hands, and I rejoice in Your deeds of mercy for me (Psalm 92:5).

I call on the Lord my God in my time of need (Psalm 50:15).

I am satisfied with the goodness of your house, the holiness of your temple (Psalm 65:4).

God, You make Your way straight and plain before me (Psalm 5:8).

I believe that I shall look upon the goodness of the Lord in the land of the living (Psalm 27:13).

I have mercy, unfailing love, compassion, and forgiveness from my God (Psalm 51).

All the promises of God to me are sure and true (Psalm 12:7).

I love the Lord because he has heard my voice and my pleas for mercy (Psalm 116:1).

God governs me with justice and equity (Psalm 9:9).

For as high as the heavens are above the earth, so great is His steadfast love toward me because I reverence Him and love Him (Psalm 103:11).

God, You are my saving shield and Your right hand upholds me (Psalm 18:36).

In peace I will both lie down and sleep for you alone, O, Lord, make me dwell in safety (Psalm 4:8).

I delight in the Lord, and He will give me the desires of my heart in due time (Psalm 37:4).

God is the strength of my heart and my portion forever (Psalm 72:26).

God will instruct me in the way that I should go (Psalm 25:12).

The law of the Lord is perfect and it refreshes my soul (Psalm 19:8).

I shall behold your face in righteousness; when I awake, I shall be satisfied with your likeness (Psalm 17:15).

I delight in the law of the Lord, and on His law I meditate day and night (Psalm 1:2).

The Lord is King, robed in splendor, and He makes my world firm and secure (Psalm 93:1).

Goodness and mercy shall follow me all the days of my life, and I shall dwell in the house of the Lord forever (Psalm 23:6).

God's mercy towards me never fails (Psalm 136:2).

I walk in integrity because God has redeemed me and taken pity upon me (Psalm 26:11).

The Lord hears my every prayer (Psalm 6:10).

I sing to God joyfully and praise His Holy Name (Psalm 98:4).

I am richly blessed in the Lord my God (Psalm 21:7).

God rules His people with justice and His world with His constancy (Psalm 96:13).

He guides me in the right path for His Name's sake (Psalm 23:3).

I sing to the Lord a new song for He has done wondrous things for me (Psalm 97:1).

I wait for the Lord with courage; I am stouthearted and wait for Him (Psalm 27:14).

Only in You, Oh, God, does my soul rest secure (Psalm 62:1).

I dwell in the house of the Lord forever (Psalm 27:4).

CHAPTER 11

God Changes Our Feelings and Our Life

Feelings[40] are what run our lives. We feel happy today, sad tomorrow, and jealous the day after that. We have no peace, no joy, no gratefulness, nor any consistency whatsoever. It's a frustrating way to live. Jesus wants our lives to be better than this.

We are double-minded, having absolutely no idea what we feel at any given time. This double-mindedness is the problem James 1:4–8 warns against. And if we take time to feel what we feel, we have no clue how to change it, even though we are perfectly aware those feelings are violating God's Holy Law (Romans 8:5–9, 12–14). Every one of the Ten Commandments is broken first by a thought or a feeling, and then in word and deed (Isaiah 1:16–17a). No one commits murder without a feeling precipitating the action, whether it is an outright murderous thought or the act itself is underpinned by anger, hatred, and unforgiveness—all of which are emotions. Karol Truman's thoughts on single-mindedness are succinct:

> Another way to describe this phenomenon is that we become integrat-ed—bringing together the thinking-conscious left brain with the feel-ing sub-conscious right brain—so that the two sides of the brain are no longer separate, but have become a whole, compatible unit. When we establish this unity, real power is created.[41]

---

40 Two different and specific meanings are defined for the words **emotions** and **feelings**. While I don't necessarily disagree with the distinction between them, the nuances of the two words are finite. I, therefore, use them interchangeably for the readability of my work.

41 Truman, *Feeling Buried Alive Never Die*, 61.

When we combine the power of God's Word with the single-mindedness that Truman is speaking about, it truly is a force to be reckoned with in the Kingdom.

Even if you knew absolutely nothing more about EFT's tapping on your acupuncture points technique, and you simply did that process of feeling and tapping day in and day out around every negative thought that entered your head or every negative memory or event, you could find yourself in a much improved emotional space.

If, however, you desire a process that is more concrete with specific steps to help you understand how to do the tapping, why we do the tapping, and what we should expect as we move forward in our emotional healing, then you have much more to learn about the tapping technique.

Sometimes, the dark, gloomy, painful thoughts that go through our mind could be leading us down a path our Savior doesn't want us to go. When we can no longer stand the emotional pain, we may become addicted to alcohol, drugs, illicit sex, pornography, overeating or other addictions that will distract us even momentarily from our painful thoughts.

That's what we do when we experience emotional pain—we run from it, as fast as we can. It hurts too much. The pain rules our life completely. We have no idea how to make our mind stop thinking about what we want to forget. For some of us, we have tried counseling. For others, we have drugs to quiet down the anxiousness around a painful memory. Some people have anxiousness and fear in their daily life for what seems no apparent reason. When these emotions plague us, we hunt and hunt for the cause, hoping God will reveal what is bothering us. Sometimes, He does reveal the problem; other times, He doesn't seem to answer us, leaving us to figure it all out on our own, which leaves us feeling even more isolated than ever.

When we can't shake that aloneness, anxiousness, and fear in our life—and all our coping mechanisms have failed us—we often find ourselves turning to other people and substitutes to distract us from feeling at all. Those substitutes, again, include alcohol, drugs, sex, pornography, overeating, daredevil/extreme stunts, gambling, and procrastination—anything that numbs out our mind, so we stop thinking the negative emotional thoughts that harass us daily.

Numbing out keeps us in what we think is control. If we don't think about something, we don't have to deal with it. The problem with using addictive behaviors to keep us from feeling any emotions is that those behaviors then begin to run our life just like the emotional overwhelm did. We trade one problem in life for another. In the end, both problems still exist.

It is very possible, however, that your negative thoughts aren't your fault. Listen to my words again: if you have been emotionally, physically, or sexually abused by someone else, then your repetitive, self-deprecating, angry, unforgiving thoughts and actions are not your fault! BUT—and this is a HUGE BUT—YOU are responsible for allowing God to help you deal with them.

If you have confessed negative thoughts and actions, God has already forgiven you. Often, though, satan continues to torment you with the same overwhelming thoughts in an attempt to keep you from moving into the glorious grace God has waiting for you. God has a plan for your life. He's always had a plan, a job He needs you to fulfill for His Kingdom here on earth. But He also needs you to step out in faith and ask Him for healing—a healing that will free you to do this special job He has ordained for you.

Quite possibly, EFT may help you get your life back. Earlier emotional distress isn't your fault. Today, your subconscious mind, as God created it, is simply trying its best to keep you safe from another round of rejection or hurt.

So now, it's time to allow God to change those decade-old feelings, removing them from the very cells of your body, where all cellular memory lives. Your DNA continues to be affected by the stress of earlier events, which still play out today—in the present—by your subconscious mind. The conscious mind says it all happened in the past, but the subconscious mind overrides the conscious mind every time—thinking yesterday is today!

Dr. Lipton states this well:

> "The conscious mind can also think forward and backward in time, while the subconscious mind is always operating in the present moment."[42]

God can change your feelings about the past. One of His transformational tools is Emotional Freedom Techniques—EFT. When old feelings are neutralized, God changes your life, often putting you on a path to emotional freedom, joy, peace, and love. His Word is true. It all can happen as written in Scripture. You can have

---

42 Lipton, *The Biology of Belief*, 139.

the Fruits of the Holy Spirit: joy, peace, patience, love, kindness, goodness, faithfulness, and self-control.

Praise be to God the Father Who gives us all good things! Amen.

I invite you to visit my website at http://www.eftforchristians.com. Search my site thoroughly. It is jam-packed with ideas and thoughts on Christian EFT, classes, blog, reading list, resources, and so much more. You can also purchase my books on my site if you reside within the US. Overseas shipping is not currently available through my site.

Contact me at EFTforChristians@gmail.com with questions or comments. I'd enjoy hearing about your tapping success stories. Perhaps, I might include your story or case study in a forthcoming book in my *EFT for Christians* book series.

Join our EFT for Christians Discussion Group on Facebook: https://www.facebook.com/groups/352652964926202/.

I also invite you to subscribe to my EFT for Christians YouTube Channel. Learn even more specifics about Christian EFT through current and upcoming videos: https://www.youtube.com/channel/UCmxsHG9CFSWot3rDZac2rSw.

With this, I will end this third book in the *EFT for Christians* book series with two more tapping case studies. Enjoy them, and God bless your emotional healing journey!

CASE STUDY: TAPPING FOR EMOTIONAL EATING – "SUGAR IS MY EMOTIONAL REGULATOR"

Beth and I had been tapping together for several months when the following sessions took place. Her primary issue was she wanted to get to the bottom of her binge eating habits and unhealthy food choices.

After opening in prayer, Beth began describing her relationship with her father. Using the "Tell the Story Technique," she tapped as she described the feelings of sadness, loneliness, and longing that characterized her relationship with him when she was growing up. Her parents divorced when she was young, and she saw her father only twice a year. He lived out of state and he bought her excessive amounts of candy and sweets to eat as they drove along in his truck during his infrequent visits.

She recalled that on one occasion when they went to a movie and he bought her candy bars, a large bucket of popcorn, and a large soft drink. She said she "consumed all of that sugar in as little as 30 minutes." This was the norm for her dad and typically what he provided for her to eat. He overfed her every time they were together. She said, "This type of eating behavior was his way of having fun, and he wanted her to have fun, too." To him, that meant "he had to feed me a lot of sugar or I wouldn't be happy." According to Beth, his thought process was, "Sugar is what makes me happy, it is what will make her happy, and it will make her like me if I give her all she wants."

As a young child, Beth had a prepaid phone calling card, which she used to call her father every day after school. Her typical routine was to escape in her mind to a place that was with him, longing for his next visit or that next phone call. In a previous session, she had described the sense of longing she felt every day on her way home from school, as she hoped against hope that she'd see her father's truck parked in the driveway at her house, since his visits were always unpredictable and unplanned. Beth had felt both angry and sad during the previous session, and as she began to talk and tap at the beginning of this session, her anger rose to the surface once again.

Beth had connected her cravings for sugar and sweets with her familial relationships in our previous sessions. In this session, she was particularly aware of the pattern established by eating sugar and sweets while visiting with her dad as a young girl. Through tapping, she came to realize that despite her fantasies about her dad, he was truly incapable of having the kind of relationship with her that she had been longing for.

At one point during our session, she said, "Despite what he taught me, and what I learned as a child, there's got to be a way to overcome this—but it's hard to do. I know the Lord can do anything, and I've been praying for this to be released and be gone, but it feels like it's tied and twisted into me. I want to get to the root cause."

When I invited Beth to tune into the physical sensations associated with the idea that something was "tied and twisted" into her emotional eating, she experienced a cognitive shift, realizing that her "emotional eating is somehow connected with not wanting to be responsible," and that "there is a grieving process that needs to take place."

Beth said, "I know this sounds like laziness and passivity, but I don't want to be responsible. I've tried. Why do I have to do all of this on my own?" As she continued tapping, however, Beth realized, "No one is going to rescue me. Dad is incompetent, Mom's not going to do it." She also observed "it's just not their job to care for me anymore. And there is no way to get back the care I deserved but lost as a child." She asked, "Why have I been trying to get the care that I deserved from them as a child when I am now capable of giving care to myself?"

She stated that she now felt "ready to be responsible in a whole new way—to be responsible for self-care, for past sin, for being a blamer in a way that takes the responsibility off me" and "not to act out anymore because I'm blaming."

Beth described spending years "expecting a rescuer, always waiting for something—for someone else to do things for me," all the while tapping and Telling her Story.

As we continued to tap, Beth began putting the pieces of her story together in a new way, understanding that for her, "eating takes the place of relationships" just as it had in her relationship with her dad. She realized that when she's "eating healthy and not eating sugar," she tends to plan more, and to be in relationships more. She said, "Food is my substitute," just as it had been when she was as a child when her dad wasn't there.

This insight led Beth to a place of greater compassion for herself. Tears streamed down her face as she felt "sadness for the girl who, for years of her life (ages 5 to 18), didn't want anything else other than to see her dad." Once again, I asked her to be aware of the physical sensations associated with her deep feelings of sadness; she described feeling "a rush of warmth from below her chest to her waist" as she "pictured herself in survival mode," remembering how she waited for him, waited for his phone calls, and fantasized about him coming to visit her. Insightfully, she said the sensation of warmth in her stomach felt "like a sugar high"—it was the same feeling of anticipation associated with seeing her dad.

Beth was stunned by this realization of her own sense of sadness, loss, and pain, yet she also acknowledged that this connection revealed the truth of a "nagging, constant sense of depression and sadness" she had felt in the past.

We tapped on specific statements such as "Why me? It's not fair," and "Why don't I have a dad?" We tapped on her sense of shame, her negative feelings about herself, and her feelings of abandonment as a child growing up. Experiencing yet another cognitive shift, Beth realized that when she eats sugar, she doesn't feel these painful feelings.

However, she also realized "sugar always brings a crash after the high." Knowing that eating sugar makes her feel even worse, Beth said, "I feel ashamed for having to control my emotions that way."

Suddenly, she recalled going to a local candy store and buying whatever candy she wanted and binging on it every day as a child at home without parental supervision in the summer. During the school year, she ate candy and ice cream cones from the school vending machines every day for lunch and then crashed afterward, feeling depressed and asking herself, "Why do I eat that stuff when it makes me feel terrible?" She recalled hating herself for eating this way every day, but feeling weak and incapable of caring for herself, realizing that her behavior was "destructive," and saying to herself, "Don't do this; all I am doing is hurting myself" and asking, "Why can't I take care of myself?"

We tapped on her sense of defeat in this area, and her feeling that change is impossible, although she knows that all things are possible with God. At that point, Beth had another sudden realization, stating, "It's feelings. Feelings are what I'm scared of. No one listened to my feelings about missing my dad and feeling neglected. No one taught me about what to do with my feelings. I hate feelings. I am so afraid of feelings."

At that moment, she made the connection — "Sugar is my emotional regulator! Whenever I feel lonely, left out, sad or stressed sugar is my emotional regulator."

We discussed this important insight and spent a few minutes talking about healthy ways to process emotions, including tapping. Because Beth and I had been working together for several months at that point, and we were near the end of the session, I suggested that she put a sign on her sugar bowl that says "Emotional Regulator," which introduced some celebratory humor as we thanked God for Beth's important cognitive shifts during the session.

When I followed up with Beth via email a few days later, she wrote, "I now have more awareness of what I'm actually doing and eating—instead of being on auto-pilot and eating as a reaction. Also, I can give myself more grace. And I love myself more than I did before because I can see the deep connections I have with food, and I can see that I'm NOT weak and I'm NOT a failure, but that food was all I had. I also see that food is NOT all I have now. I have many resources at my fingertips that provide other, more healthy ways to process emotions or cope with emotions that don't involve food. Obviously, it's a process, but I'm headed down the right path. Also, I understand why none of the "behavior modification" type diet plans ever worked; the problem was way deeper than behavior. Praise the Lord. I'm grateful to Him.

In the next session, Beth and I continued to tap on issues related to her emotional eating and her relationship with her dad. This time, when I asked Beth to tune into the physical sensations she was experiencing, she described a sensation like "thick rough, brown ropes the size of three basketballs knotted up in her stomach." She said the ropes felt "like they weighed twenty pounds, and they were associated with feeling shame, frustration, helplessness, hopelessness, and self-hatred. Returning to themes from the previous session she said, "There's no one here to help me. I have to do this on my own."

As we tapped on all of these thoughts, feelings, and emotions, Beth recalled wanting to isolate herself at school, rather than sitting with the other children at lunch. She said, "I had two choices. I could go off by myself and eat, or I could sit with my peers. I didn't want to be around people." She recalled thinking, "No one in my household likes me, so why would anybody else like me?" Recalling the sense of isolation and loneliness she felt as a child, Beth said, "food was her only comfort, and somehow it seemed to help."

As we tapped, Beth's feelings of loneliness intensified. She got in touch with her longing to connect with others in relationships while also feeling "scared," and even "terrified" to do so. Beth felt this feeling of terror "everywhere"—in her head, shoulders, back, torso—describing it as a heavy feeling and a desire to fight or flee.

As she acknowledged these feelings while tapping, we also tapped in scriptural affirmations since Beth professed she was "ready to release all of her shame, and give these feelings to the Lord." We acknowledged that Jesus bore her shame, and this is no longer a burden she needs to carry. We affirmed God is her comforter, her companion, and an ever-present help in times of trouble. She reaffirmed her hope is in Him, that He is sufficient to provide for all of her needs, that He will guide her, and that He will help her in a way that her earthly father never could. We asked Him to fill her with His light and His love, and acknowledged His faithfulness, trusting that He will continue to bring healing in all of these areas of her life.

Feeling calmer as we continued to tap, Beth found herself experiencing the "sense of excitement" she felt as she anticipated her dad's arrival when she was younger, while "waiting for him to come, thinking about the food." She described a "tingling sensation in her head," which felt like "wanting to connect."

As the session drew to a close, Beth said she connected the excitement she feels when she anticipates eating sugary foods with the longing to be with her dad that she experienced as a young girl. Beth said she had never seen this connection so clearly before, and we ended the session on a note of renewed hope, knowing He who began a good work in her will be faithful to complete it.

Several days later, she wrote, "I had a big aha moment yesterday. It's not food I have a problem with, it's feelings. And when I look at it that way, it doesn't feel impossible to overcome. And I'm able to give myself soooo much more grace because I can TOTALLY understand why a person with my childhood experiences would have a problem with emotions and feelings. It makes sense for the first time in my life. I always focused on the eating (the branches) instead of the feelings (the root)."

So I'm releasing all of my emotions to the Lord. He created them; He can help me with them. And as I heal, I can be a better vessel for Him to work through to minister to His people. These are such exciting times."

In a subsequent follow-up email, Beth wrote, "Now I think the Lord is saying it's even deeper than the feelings... it's the trauma... and the memories. I guess He will just keep revealing more and more. But I think I'm headed down the right path, hand in hand with the Lord."

Laurie Heyl, LCSW
LHEYL.LCSW@gmail.com
EFT-EnergyInMotion.com

EFT works just this way. As the Holy Spirit feels you are able and ready, He allows more layers of emotional pain to be released and tapped on. Remember, He will never allow you more than you can handle (1 Corinthians 10:13).

VIOLET'S STORY: WHAT IF I'M NOT SAVED?

By Cathy Reiling

Violet, a striking 72-year-old Southern Belle with a strong Louisiana accent came to me presenting back pain and unprocessed grief around her husband's death 2 years prior. She was working on adjusting to being a widow, living alone and dealing with her own medical issues. We had worked through several sessions together on many of her traumatic events, such as her husband's unsuccessful surgeries, strokes, and incorrect diagnoses during the 2 years preceding his death. We cleared much grief and anger around many events from the previous 4 years, along with establishing her new role as a widow. Violet and her husband were both committed Christians and very involved in their church. She had and continues to have a strong support group of friends and family.

In one of our later sessions, Violet discussed a recent dream she had, reminding her of a fearful event from her childhood. She was raised as a Southern Baptist and was a very obedient child, for the most part, always desiring to please and honor her father and mother. Her dad was very strict, and her mother was silent regarding the disciplining that went along with their restrictive religious ways. Violet attended church every Sunday and midweek Bible classes. She wasn't permitted to participate in some of the activities that her schoolmates were, such as dancing and card games. Violet told me about a special church revival meeting she and her family had attended, and she had some very unsure feelings around it. I asked her permission to pray to begin the session as we always did, and she agreed. We began thanking God and asking His Holy Spirit to lead and guide our session, and to bring to remembrance memories and areas that were ready to receive healing.

Immediately, a scene came to her mind in which she is about the age of 12, sitting in a church pew feeling very unsure. I asked her if she could put the scene on pause and describe it to me. I asked her to tap on her collarbone point and inquiring how high the emotion was. She said it was about a 6 on the SUDS scale. As she began to describe the scene to me, she could see her younger self wearing a cream-colored lace dress with baby blue ribbon and her new black shiny shoes. Her family was also sitting on the same pew further down from her. She said she felt like she had a big secret and could not tell anybody. She was continually tapping on her collarbone point and switching back to her side of the hand and her body was remaining calm for the most part as she described the scene to me. I asked her what emotion was connected to this big secret, and she replied that she was hiding the belief that she wasn't sure if she was saved or not. She said she felt like a backslider and that something was wrong with her. The biggest part was she could not tell anyone because she also felt unworthy and was afraid she would disappoint her parents if she were not saved. No way could she tell them this secret. She remembered struggling with this fear for a few years, since the time in her Bible class a few years prior when the teacher had the students go through the steps of salvation, and Violet did not think she did one of the steps or did them out of order. And now, during this altar call at the revival meeting, the threat of not being saved was overwhelming, and Violet felt very unworthy and afraid. Her SUDS number increased to 9 and, at that time, we tapped a few rounds using the basic recipe, addressing the fear of keeping the secret, and how disappointed her parents would be if they knew. Her SUDS came down to a 3 after two to three rounds of tapping.

Violet continued, stating she definitely had asked Jesus into her heart, BUT she was not sure if she "did the salvation steps in the right order." Thus she was not sure if she was saved. When she told me that, it was the first time she had told anybody because she was very afraid she might go to Hell. She believed that everyone in the revival meeting was saved, but her. There was an altar call, and she was afraid to go up. I asked her to keep the scene frozen. She felt she HAD to keep her secret. We did a tapping round on following the exact steps, not missing one thing while doing the steps out of order. Her SUDS came down from 9 to 6. So with the scene frozen, I asked her to see if she could see Jesus in the meeting, and she said she could sense his presence very close to her child self in the pew. I asked her to bring her adult self into the scene, on the pew, and to have a conversation with her younger self while continuing to tap on her body points.

The adult Violet was very sad that the 12-year-old had to feel such unworthiness and fear. We did a tapping round on the sadness she felt, which dropped her 6 SUDs level to 3. I asked her to let Jesus lead her in what she wanted to say to her younger self and to allow the 12-year-old to respond and express a reply.

Violet said to her younger self, "I know you are afraid, and you do not believe you are saved, and that you do not want to disappoint your parents by telling them. You have kept this secret a very long time, and you do not have to keep it anymore. Jesus loves you so much, and you ARE saved, and you do not have to question your salvation any longer. The fact that you asked him into your heart is the main step that counts. The order of the other steps you took earlier did not matter. You do not need to live in fear of disappointing your mom and dad because they are very proud of you. You are free from keeping this secret because you are, in fact, saved. Jesus will be here for you for the rest of your life, and He does not want you to be afraid." Violet was lightly crying while she talked to her younger self. She continued tapping. I asked if there was anything the 12-year-old would like to say. She said that the 12-year-old was smiling and Jesus was holding both of them, and they were all smiling, feeling very accepted and comforted. The 12-year-old Violet also knew she did not have to answer that altar call, and she could go home feeling free from that burden of keeping a secret. She looked over at her mom and dad, and they both smiled at her. She knew all was well. The younger Violet said, "Thank you for being here." Violet told her younger self she would always be here for her.

Violet felt so relieved that all the fear and unworthiness were gone. She felt closer to God and was glad her children were not raised in such a strict religious home, but rather in a church and home that extends the grace and the love of God. She was reminded of the Scripture verse "for it is by grace you have been saved through faith, and this not from yourselves; it is the gift of God, not by works, so that no one can boast (Ephesians 2:8–9).

We ended in prayer and Scripture, thanking God for His continuing to work His good pleasure in Violet.

> "for it is God who works in you to will and to act in order to fulfill His good purpose." Philippians 2:13

"And being confident of this, that he who began a good work in you will carry it on to completion until the day of Christ Jesus." Philippians 1:6

Violet shared how relieved she felt after this session, and how surprised she was that the event had still bothered her years after knowing the love and grace of God from her adult understanding of salvation. She felt more connected with herself than before the session started but concerned about how many people are questioning their salvation due to similar beliefs and childhood events.

I shared one of my favorite Scriptures with her:

"For though we live in the flesh, we do not wage war according to the flesh. The weapons of our warfare are not the weapons of the world. Instead, they have the power to demolish strongholds. We tear down arguments, and every presumption set up against the knowledge of God, and we take captive every thought to make it obedient to Christ." 2 Corinthians 4:3–5

EFT tapping is a tool we can use to help the body and brain balance and remain calm under the memory of traumatic events. It then can allow us to work very effectively in taking down these strongholds of false beliefs that hold us captive and prevent us from receiving the blessings and peace God has for us. I also shared with Violet how we are to be renewed in the spirit of our minds; and to put on the new self, created to be like God in true righteousness and holiness (Ephesians 4:23).

It can be difficult at times to put on the new self when these old false beliefs are interfering with our new desires to love and receive from God. Tapping has helped in taking these beliefs and thoughts captive for Violet, helping her to put on the new self.

Violet left the session very grateful for all that God has done for her, and she reports she uses tapping daily in her prayer time. It helps her to get deeper, at times, than before she knew about tapping.

In a more recent update, Violet has embraced being a widow and enjoys her life—doing artwork, exercising, and walks on the beach. Her back discomfort is manageable with exercise, and her love of God has never been stronger.

Cathy Reiling is a Certified Clinical EFT and Matrix Re-Imprinting Practitioner near Seattle, WA. She and her husband were co-pastors of a non-denominational church in the Pacific Northwest where she counseled married couples and taught classes on "Communion with God" and "Discover your Spiritual Gifts."

Cathy Reiling
Christian Certified EFT Practitioner
cathyreiling@gmail.com

ABOUT THE AUTHOR

SHERRIE RICE SMITH, R.N. (RETIRED)

Sherrie has more than four decades in nursing, which includes work in medical-surgical, home health, and hospice care. Sherrie has an intense interest in all things related to biology, physiology, psychology, and quantum mechanics. These interests allow for an understanding of the efficaciousness of Emotional Freedom Techniques. Her personal experience with EFT is based on her own life story, giving her an even greater appreciation of how well EFT can bring both physical and emotional healing when coupled with prayer and the knowledge that Jesus heals.

Sherrie holds two EFT certifications, mentors Christian EFT Practitioners and students, and teaches certification classes, levels 1 and 2, for EFTUniverse. She is also the author of *EFT for Christians*, originally published in 2015.

Sherrie and her husband, Brad, reside in Milwaukee and travel extensively throughout the United States. Please join Sherrie on Facebook at www.facebook.com/groups/352652964926202/ or www.facebook.com/groups/307887129394873/ or subscribe to Sherrie's EFT for Christians blog at http://eftforchristian.blogspot.com/

BIBLIOGRAPHY

Church, Dawson Ph.D. *The Genie in Your Genes: Epigenetic Medicine and the New Biology of Intention.* Santa Rosa, CA: Energy Psychology Press, 2014.

Church, D., Yount, G, & Brooks, A.J. 2012. "The effect of emotional freedom techniques on stress biochemistry: A randomized controlled trial." *Journal of Nervous and Mental Disease*, 200(10), 891-896. doi. 10.1097/NMD.0b013e31826b9fc1.

Clemons-Jones, Rev. Kymberly. *Cured But Not Healed: How to Experience Deeper Faith on Your Journey with God.* Prospect, KY: Professional Woman Publishing, LLC, 2012.

Dispenza, Dr. Joe. *Breaking the Habit of Being Yourself: How to Lose Your Mind and Create a New One.* Carlsbad, CA: Hay House, 2012.

Grudem, Wayne. *Systematic Theology: An Introduction to Biblical Doctrine.* Grand Rapids, MI: Zondervan, 1994.

Jeeves, Malcolm and Berry, R.J. *Science, Life and Christian Belief.* Grand Rapids, MI: Baker Books, 1998.

Leaf, Dr. Caroline. *Who Switched off My Brain?* Dallas, TX: Switch on Your Brain USA Inc., 2008.

Leaf, Dr. Caroline. *How to Switch on Your Brain: The Key to Peak Happiness, Thinking, and Health.* Grand Rapids, MI: Baker Books, 2013.

Lipton, Bruce H., Ph.D. *The Biology of Belief: Unleashing the Power of Consciousness, Matter and Miracles.* Carlsbad, CA: Hay House, 2008.

Levine, Peter A. *Waking the Tiger Healing Trauma.* Berkeley, CA: North Atlantic Books, 1997.

Maté, Gabor M.D. *When the Body Says NO: Exploring the Stress-Disease Connection.* Hoboken, NJ: John Wiley & Sons, 2003.

Myss, Caroline, PhD. *Anatomy of the Spirit: The Seven Stages of Power and Healing.* New York: Three Rivers Press, 1997.

Truman, Karol K. *Feeling Buried Alive Never Die.* St. George, UT: Olympus Distributing, 2011.

Van der Kolk, Bessel, M.D. *The Body Keeps the Score: Brain, Mind, and Body in the Healing of Trauma.* New York: Viking, 2014.

Virkler Kayembe, Charity and Rice Smith, Sherrie. *EFT for Christians: Tapping in God's Peace and Joy.* Travelers Rest, SC: True Potential, 2016.

Wardle, Terry. *Wounded: How You Can Find Inner Wholeness and Healing in Him.* Camp Hill, PA: Christian Publications, 1994.

Wolynn, Mark. *It Didn't Start with You: How Inherited Family Trauma Shapes Who We Are and How to End the Cycle.* New York: Viking, 2016.

Made in the USA
Columbia, SC
25 November 2017